D0153194

THE AMBASSADORS

Consciousness, Culture, Poetry

TWAYNE'S MASTERWORK STUDIES

Robert Lecker, General Editor

THE AMBASSADORS

Consciousness, Culture, Poetry

Richard A. Hocks

TWAYNE PUBLISHERS
An Imprint of Simon & Schuster Macmillan
New York

PRENTICE HALL INTERNATIONAL
London Mexico City New Delhi Singapore Sydney Toronto

Twayne's Masterwork Series No. 165

The Ambassadors: Consciousness, Culture, Poetry
Richard A. Hocks

Twayne Publishers
An Imprint of Simon & Schuster Macmillan
1633 Broadway
New York, New York 10019

Library of Congress Cataloging-in-Publication Data

Hocks, Richard A., 1936–
    The ambassadors : consciousness, culture, poetry / Richard A.
Hocks.
        p.   cm. — (Twayne's masterwork studies : no. 165)
    Includes bibliographical references and index.
    ISBN 0-8057-8371-7 (alk. paper). — ISBN 0-8057-8573-6 (pbk. :
alk. paper)
        1. James, Henry, 1843–1916. Ambassadors.   I. Title.   II. Series.
PS2116.A53H63   1997
813'.4—dc21   97-4004
                                                                                          CIP

10 9 8 7 6 5 4 3 2

Printed in the United States of America

For Dr. Rick, Dr. Elaine, Dr. Mary

Contents

The late James (of *The Ambassadors, Wings of the Dove,* and *Golden Bowl*).

Alvin Langdon Cobwin

Note on the References and Acknowledgments

Parenthetical references to *The Ambassadors* are to *The Novels and Tales of Henry James,* vols. XXI–XXII (New York: Charles Scribner's Sons, 1909). This is the New York Edition, and I choose this text because it incorporates James's last revisions. Unlike some early James works (such as *Daisy Miller* or, say, *Roderick Hudson*), there is no dispute over which edition of *The Ambassadors* is the preferred text; that is, there is not the same disparity of style between the first publication and the New York Edition, published 30 years later. Throughout this study I have cited volumes XXI and XXII as I and II, respectively, which is common practice in James scholarship.

There are many "teaching" editions of *The Ambassadors,* most of which reprint the text of the New York Edition. I have chosen not to cite one of these because there is no particular reason to favor one over another. In the bibliography I list the Norton Critical Edition and the Penguin Classics edition: the first has the most scholarly apparatus, the second is less expensive but well edited. Other equally desirable and economical texts of *The Ambassadors* include editions by Washington Square, Bantam Books, New American Library, and Oxford World's Classics, among others. Throughout the course of my argument I have endeavored to keep the reader informed of the structural division of the novel from which specific citations come.

Whoever writes about *The Ambassadors* owes a major debt of gratitude to the novel's many previous commentators. There is no better community of scholars and critics than those who write about

James. In my argument, I have already emphasized works by Paul B. Armstrong, Daniel M. Fogel, Susan M. Griffin, Michael Seidel, and Dorothea Krook in particular. I am also very grateful to the Research Council, University of Missouri, for recommending to the office of the provost a research leave to advance this study. Finally, as always, my thanks goes to my wife, Elaine, for her great support and willingness to reshape many plans to accommodate this task.

Chronology

1843	Henry James born 15 April at 21 Washington Place, New York City, to Henry James Sr. and Mary Robertson Walsh. William James born 18 months earlier. Family lives abroad in England and France from 1843 to 1845.
1847	Family lives at 58 W. 14th Street, New York City, where frequent visitors include Horace Greeley, William Cullen Bryant, and Ralph Waldo Emerson.
1855	Family departs 17 June for three-year stay in Europe, where Henry attends school and is privately tutored in Geneva, London, and Paris.
1858	Family returns to America and settles in Newport, Rhode Island, where Henry studies art with the painter John La Forge.
1859	Family returns to Europe. Henry studies engineering in Geneva and German in Bonn.
1861	Outbreak of the Civil War. While fighting a stable fire in October, Henry suffers his "obscure hurt," a back injury that keeps him out of the war.
1862	Henry enters Harvard Law School.
1863	Leaves Harvard to devote himself to writing.
1864	Family settles in Boston and then in Cambridge, Massachusetts. His first story, "A Tragedy of Error," is published, unsigned. *North American Review* begins publishing his book reviews.
1865	The *Atlantic Monthly* publishes James's first signed story, "The Story of a Year." James vacations in the White Mountains with his cousin Minnie Temple and Oliver Wendell Holmes Jr., future Supreme Court justice.

1866	Begins his lifelong friendship with editor and novelist William Dean Howells (the eventual "source" for *The Ambassadors*).
1869	Travels alone to Europe, where he meets Charles Darwin, George Eliot, John Ruskin, Edward Burne-Jones, and others.
1870	Minnie Temple dies at 24 and becomes the prototype for James's "American Girl," embodied in such characters as Daisy Miller, Isabel Archer, and Milly Theale. Henry returns to Cambridge in May and visits Ralph Waldo Emerson in Concord for a few days.
1871	Henry's first novel, *Watch and Ward,* is serialized in the *Atlantic Monthly.*
1872	From May to October travels in Europe with his aunt Kate and sister Alice. In Paris he befriends James Russell Lowell and guides Emerson through the Louvre.
1873	Spends most of the year in Italy and for the first time earns enough money from writing to support himself.
1874	In September he returns to America.
1875	Lives and writes in New York City; first three books published: *Transatlantic Sketches, A Passionate Pilgrim and Other Tales,* and *Roderick Hudson.* Returns to Paris in November, where he enjoys the literary society of Ivan Turgenev, Gustave Flaubert, Emile Zola, Alphonse Daudet, Guy de Maupassant, Edmond de Goncourt, and others.
1876	Establishes residence in London at 3 Bolton Street, Piccadilly.
1877	His novel *The American* is published. Meets Robert Browning.
1878	"Daisy Miller," published in *Cornhill Magazine,* establishes his transatlantic fame and celebrity. Meets Alfred Lord Tennyson, George Meredith, and James McNeill Whistler (whose Parisian home later figures prominently in *The Ambassadors*). *French Poets and Novelists* is published and *The Europeans* is serialized.
1879	"Daisy Miller" published in book form as *Daisy Miller: A Study/An International Episode/Four Meetings. The Madonna of the Future and Other Tales* is also published. Establishes friendship with Robert Louis Stevenson. Publishes *Hawthorne,* his first book-length study of an American writer.
1880	*Confidence* and *Washington Square* are published. Serialization of *The Portrait of a Lady* begins in October in England in *Macmillan's Magazine* and in America in the *Atlantic Monthly.*

Chronology

nations, the first of his collection of tales with a separate title, is published.

1896   *The Spoils of Poynton* is serialized in the *Atlantic Monthly.* *Embarrassments* (tales) is published.

1897   *The Spoils of Poynton* is published in book form. *What Maisie Knew* is published. Begins friendship with Joseph Conrad. Due to writer's cramp, he begins to dictate fiction to a typist, which he will continue to do for the duration of his career. Establishes himself at Lamb House in Rye, England, which will become his principal residence.

1898   *The Two Magics: The Turn of the Screw/Covering End* is published. *The Turn of the Screw* becomes his biggest popular success since *Daisy Miller.* Publishes *In the Cage.*

1899   *The Awkward Age* is published. Sees brother William for first time in six years. Meets sculptor Hendrik Christian Anderson. James B. Pinker becomes his literary agent.

1900   *The Soft Side* (tales) is published. Begins *The Ambassadors.*

1901   Publishes *The Sacred Fount* (its technique opposes that of *The Ambassadors*). Completes *The Ambassadors* and begins *The Wings of the Dove.* Shaves off beard worn since Civil War.

1902   *The Wings of the Dove* is published. Writes "The Beast in the Jungle."

1903   *The Ambassadors* is published, first in serial form by *The North American Review,* then in America by Harper and in England by Methuen. *The Better Sort* (tales) are also published. Meets Edith Wharton.

1904   *The Golden Bowl,* James's last major novel, is published. After a 20-year absence, he begins in August a yearlong tour of the United States. Visits Wharton, meets President Theodore Roosevelt, lectures on Balzac.

1905   Returns to England. Starts revisions of novels for the New York Edition of *The Novels and Tales of Henry James* (24 volumes, 1907–1909). Publishes *English Hours* and *The Question of Our Speech* (essays).

1906   Continues revising and begins writing 18 prefaces for the New York Edition.

1907   *The American Scene* is published. Travels in France with Wharton. Visits Italy for the last time.

1907–1909   The New York Edition is published; *The Ambassadors* (1909) comprises Volumes XXI and XXII.

Chronology

1909   *Italian Hours* (travel essays) is published.

1910   Suffers a nervous breakdown. In August returns to America with failing brother William, who dies. Brother Robertson also dies. *The Finer Grain* (last and finest collection of tales) is published.

1911   Returns to England. Resides at Reform Club in London to avoid loneliness of Lamb House.

1912   Spends summer at Lamb House and sees much of Edith Wharton.

1913   Begins his autobiographies. *A Small Boy and Others* is published. Moves to 21 Carlyle Mansions, Cheyne Walk, Chelsea. Honored with a 70th-birthday tribute at which he receives such gifts as a Sargent portrait and a golden bowl. Spends summers at Lamb House.

1914   *Notes of a Son and Brother,* second volume of autobiography, and *Notes on Novelists* are published. Horrified by the war, James accepts a position as chairman of the American Volunteer Motor Ambulance Corps and visits wounded in hospitals.

1915   Becomes a British citizen in support of allies. Suffers a stroke on December 2.

1916   Receives Order of Merit from King George V on New Year's Day. Dies 28 February, two months before his 73rd birthday. His ashes are buried in the family plot in Cambridge Cemetery, Cambridge, Massachusetts. Memorial plaque laid in poets' corner of Westminster Abbey (plaque now lies alongside those commemorating T. S. Eliot and Thomas Hardy).

1917   Unfinished novels *The Ivory Tower, The Sense of the Past,* and *The Middle Years* (autobiography) are published.

1919   *Within the Rim* (last essays) is published.

1920   *The Letters of Henry James* (early Percy Lubbock edition) is published.

LITERARY AND
HISTORICAL CONTEXTS

1

The Historical Context

Henry James was 60 years old when he published *The Ambassadors* (1903), the second of his great trilogy of novels that began with *The Wings of the Dove* (1902) and ended with *The Golden Bowl* (1904). Today these works constitute the core of James's late period, or "major phase." *The Ambassadors* is also the novel James designates, in his definitive critical document, the preface to the New York Edition, "the best 'all round' of all my productions."[1] This assessment by the first major critic of fiction in America after Edgar Allan Poe still carries great weight: James clearly singled out *The Ambassadors* as a masterwork from his voluminous corpus of writings.

The novels of James's major phase did not achieve the popular or financial success of his earlier work, however, and hence his later books routinely carry the inscription "by the author of *Daisy Miller*." And yet, the three final completed novels signified the culmination of an extensive set of stages in James's five-decade-long artistic career. The first period of his work, from the mid-1860s to his first great novel, *The Portrait of a Lady* (1881), was characterized by his discovery and refinement of the international novel and tale—especially in *The American* (1877), *Daisy Miller* (1878), *An International Episode*

(1879), and *The Portrait of a Lady* (1881). Daniel M. Fogel expounds James's international fiction as follows:

> Most of [James's] novels and tales involve their protagonists in transatlantic quests for experience: new situations and unprecedented dilemmas—created by the American heroes' and heroines' immersion in European manners, culture, and civilization—lead them to new perceptions so profound that their selves are transformed.[2]

In his early period, James combined this international content with a mastery of the new post–Civil War realism. Indeed, his experiments in realistic social comedy and satire marked a turning point in American literature, taking it from the earlier Romantic Movement—the school of Poe, Cooper, Melville, and Hawthorne—to its Realist and later Naturalist phases. In particular, James studied Hawthorne's work carefully in order to extend and transform it into his own newer art of fiction.[3]

The second period of James's career, from the 1880s to 1901, reveals his divergence from the international novel and his focus instead on broad surgical critiques of society. He placed the novels of this phase in either England or America exclusively rather than depicting American characters who confront the labyrinth of Europe. Narratives that James composed during this second period include *The Bostonians* (1886) and a rich series of novels set in London or its environs: *The Princess Casamassima* (1886), *What Maisie Knew* (1897), *The Spoils of Poynton* (1897), *In the Cage* (1898), *The Awkward Age* (1899), and *The Sacred Fount* (1901). These books, although not international in theme, do show the transatlantic influence of the great continental novelists of the age, especially Ivan Turgenev, Gustave Flaubert, and Emile Zola, all of whom James knew. For although James always remained first and foremost an American writer, he came to be fluent in French and Italian and thus became a truly cosmopolitan novelist. In any case, this second group of novels exhibits a powerful satiric social consciousness—one rivaling Dickens—along with an extraordinary propensity for experimentalism in the developing genre of the novel itself.[4]

The Historical Context

After his ill-fated attempt to compose successfully for the theater in 1895 (he was booed from the stage) and his forays into the realms of the art parable and the "ghostly" studies of obsession (e.g., "The Real Thing," 1892, and *The Turn of the Screw,* 1898), James was ready to embark on his third period, from 1901 to 1916. Although he composed a final sequence of complex tales in 1910, *The Finer Grain,* and afterward penned important autobiographical volumes, it is *The Ambassadors,* together with the other two novels of the trilogy, that enunciate his pioneering dramas of consciousness with their "dense fusion of realism, naturalism, and extraordinary poetic symbolism."[5] These late novels, along with such corresponding tales as *The Beast in the Jungle* (1903) and "The Jolly Corner" (1908), became in turn a major foundation for the radical international modernism of Joseph Conrad, F. Scott Fitzgerald, Virginia Woolf, and James Joyce. They also exerted a profound influence on such poets as T. S. Eliot, Ezra Pound, and Wallace Stevens.[6] Henry James began, then, as a pioneer of realistic social comedy, then evolved by turns into a master of psychological realism, an experimenter with naturalism, an inventor of nonsupernatural, "ghostly" fiction, and, finally, a modern symbolist. In other words, as he evolved toward *The Ambassadors* and the trilogy of late novels, he mastered and in turn influenced first Victorian and then early modern fiction.

James's lifelong wish was to use the international theme of America and Europe to promote tolerance, to undermine the smug nationalistic arrogance that emanated from both sides of the Atlantic. *The Ambassadors* presents us with an American puritan, Lambert Strether, whose rich imagination impels him to develop a new sensitivity in midlife to cultural practices that go squarely against the grain of his New England ethics and that even impede his financial prospects. Yet Strether subsequently "rediscovers" his just-discarded puritanism in dramatic fashion—only to challenge himself again by remaining committed to his newer appreciation of European mores despite his personal shock and chagrin. Such twisting around of moral positioning creates, for both Strether and the reader, a double-helix–like cultural odyssey, one that suggests James's book may be a kind of spiritual autobiography. While justly admired for his great female

5

protagonists, James creates in Lambert Strether a figure we can iden-
tify with Henry James himself, the "restless analyst" of culture (a term
James used for himself in his memoir and critique of culture entitled
The American Scene, 1907).

The same novel and its companions in the trilogy are also recognized justly as the works of a very special kind of historian. Joseph
Conrad, in his 1905 essay on James entitled "An Appreciation," denominates him the "historian of fine consciences," a phrase that practically sounds as if it were coined for Strether, the ruminating protagonist of *The Ambassadors.*[7] R. P. Blackmur, in the monumental *Literary
History of the United States,* provides still another bow to the later
James as a special kind of historian. He writes perceptively of James's
"kind of reality different from both the literal record of a [William
Dean] Howells and the philosophical naturalism of [an Emile] Zola."
Blackmur further explains:

> This reality was his response to the human predicament of his
> generation—the predicament of the sensitive mind during what
> may be called the interregnum between the effective dominance
> of the old Christian-classical ideal through old European institu-
> tions and the rise to rule of the succeeding ideal, whatever history
> comes to call it.[8]

Interestingly, James's "reality" in his late period, though different from that of Howells or Zola, nevertheless incorporates key elements of these colleagues. For example, in *The Ambassadors* James
uses such foregrounding landscapes as the medieval wall at Chester or
the cathedral of Notre Dame as would do Howells proud. And his
philosophical treatment of determinism—which we shall explore
later—offers both a nod and a challenge to Zola.

The sort of nuanced historian in James that both Blackmur and
Conrad describe is addressed in a slightly different vein by Ezra
Pound, who affirmed that James's late novels constituted an eloquent
attack by a "hater of tyranny" who attempted to make "three nations
intelligible one to another" and who communicated "the recognition
of differences, of the right of differences to exist." Pound's comments
are still another motto-in-effect of *The Ambassadors* and are comple-

mented by his colleague T. S. Eliot, who proclaimed James as someone whose profundity was "more useful, more applicable to our future" than even Dostoyevsky's.[9] This anti-imperialist strain, moreover, is an important part of James's literary milieu. It can be found in such turn-of-the-century intellectuals as his brother William, for instance, whose philosophy of pragmatism is embodied throughout *The Ambassadors* (as we shall see later in this study). It is likewise found in Howells and in the late Mark Twain, specifically in the wake of the Spanish American War and the European conquests in the Philippines and elsewhere. For all his artistry Henry James was a man of his times, and in *The Ambassadors* we encounter a domestic analogue to nationalist coercion and manipulation. And we discover in the figure of the protagonist Strether a sometimes heroic, sometimes hapless, yet poignant struggle for freedom and "the right of differences to exist." When Pound and Eliot praise James as an intellectual liberal who fosters humane values in the face of a corroding social order, our first associations are perhaps with the era and ambience surrounding World War I. And yet the continuing relevance of James's humane values is registered strongly in later tributes by such well-respected writers as Stephen Spender, Lionel Trilling, and James Baldwin—whose response to James as a fighter for humanity and freedom impelled the author of *Go Tell It on the Mountain* and "Sonny's Blues" to keep a picture of James above his own writing desk as an incentive.[10]

Finally, another historical context that may shed light on *The Ambassadors* is the book's origin in a particular suggestive event, or "germ"—the term James applied in his criticism to initiating moments, episodes, or ideas in his creative process. In *The Ambassadors,* we actually have one of the best-documented cases in all of American literature of a single generative incident eventually giving rise to an American masterpiece. The incident is this: William Dean Howells stood in a Parisian garden owned by the painter James McNeill Whistler sometime in 1894 and declared poignantly to his 30-year-old *confrère* Jonathan Sturges,

> Oh, you are young, you are young—be glad of it and *live*—Live all you can: it's a mistake not to. It doesn't so much matter what

you do—but live. This place makes it all come over me. I see it now. I haven't done so—and now I'm old. It's too late. It has gone past me—I've lost it. You have time. You are young. Live![11]

That, at least, is the way James first recorded it in his notebooks on 31 October 1895, the day after young Sturges visited him and recalled the memorable incident. Howells's lament became the organic germ James used to conceive and later compose the novel. Time and time again—first in his notebooks, then in a special "Scenario" he composed for Harper's in 1900, then in two letters he wrote to Howells while working on the novel (1900–1901), then again in *The Ambassadors* itself (1903), and, finally, in his preface to the New York Edition of his collected works (1909)—James reiterates the same point: that the entire novel expanded from this initiating moment. He insists to Howells by letter that the book was "lovely—human, dramatic, international," was "exquisitely everything from the germ up," was even a case in which "nothing can exceed the closeness with which the whole fits again into its germ."[12]

Whatever else we may say about *The Ambassadors*, then, it remains the textbook model for James's theory of the creative process as a germ organically expanded into the modern "poetic" novel—the novel in which character determines incident, a reverse of Aristotle's *Poetics* during a non-Aristotelian era. That era is in fact the historical "interregnum for the human predicament in the West" of which R. P. Blackmur speaks earlier, the changeover from the "Christian-classical ideal" to the beginnings of modern secularism. If Blackmur is right, James's genetic and compositional history reaches out to meet the crossover drift in intellectual and cultural Western history itself.

2

The Importance of the Work

Critical acclaim for *The Ambassadors* has remained consistently high for more than 90 years, although *Daisy Miller* is more accessible, *The Turn of the Screw* more suspenseful and frightening, and *The Portrait of a Lady* deeply satisfactory for combining an earlier, easier prose style with key elements of the later fiction. The later James himself, incidentally, showed typical prescience by choosing *The Portrait of a Lady* (1881) just ahead of either *The Wings of the Dove* (1902) or *The Golden Bowl* (1904), calling it "the most proportioned of [my] productions after 'The Ambassadors'—which was to follow it so many years later and which has, no doubt, a superior roundness."[1] Let us consider briefly some reasons for this long-standing regard for *The Ambassadors,* first by James and ever since by many of his best readers. Most of these reasons will be reexamined later in this study in more detail.

The first, "classic" reason for the high esteem of *The Ambassadors* is that, despite its heft and amplitude, the work achieves great technical virtuosity by keeping its point of view confined within the mind of the protagonist, Lambert Strether. This feature is possibly its most significant difference from *The Portrait of a Lady*. Related to this accomplishment is James's startlingly successful realization of a character like Strether's imposing benefactor, Mrs. Newsome, even though she never physically appears in any scene but is rendered instead through Strether's reflections of or conversations about her. Another spin-off from James's restricted point of view is his use of the "ficelle" figure, someone who, in dialogue with Strether, enables him to relate crucial information that the reader would not otherwise have without an omniscient narrator. Waymarsh and Maria Gostrey, Strether's confidants, whom he meets at Chester immediately after disembarking at Liverpool, are splendid examples of the ficelle. James's skill shows all the more when Maria's role in particular becomes complicated by her losing her heart to Strether. In other words, she eventually transcends her merely ficelle function as his European guide and confidant. Such technique not only enables James to compensate for giving up his authorial omniscience but creates surprisingly new modes of flexibility as the very consequence of restriction.

The Ambassadors likewise marks the return of the international theme—or perhaps more accurately in James the international subject—so prominent in his first period. Like the poet William Blake, whose mature vision recapitulates earlier preoccupations with innocence and experience in order to evolve toward a new plane of "organized innocence," James's major-phase novel both evolves to new heights and presents new ambiguities. To accomplish this evolution he becomes stylistically more complex and marked by long periodic sentences with elliptical syntax and capacious metaphor. As with Blake, archetypal structures—so often defined as transhistorical (but never *ahistorical,* as too many critics now wrongly assume)—are themselves a major feature of the architecture of *The Ambassadors*, given its special status as a late-James work of the imagination.

Still another reason for the book's enduring importance is James's unique treatment of a classic philosophical dilemma, freedom and determinism. In keeping with his theory of the organically expanding germ, James introduces this question by placing it at the center of Strether's "germ speech" in the sculptor Gloriani's garden. When lamenting his failure to live, William Dean Howells, of course, said nothing whatever of this issue to Jonathan Sturges. But Lambert Strether utters to little Bilham,

The Affair—I mean the affair of life—couldn't, no doubt, have been different for me; for it's at the best a tin mould, either fluted or embossed, with ornamental excrescences, or else smooth and dreadfully plain, into which, a helpless jelly, one's consciousness is poured—so that one "takes" the form, as the great cook says, and is more or less compactly held by it: one lives in fine as one can. Still, one has the illusion of freedom; therefore don't be, like me, without the memory of that illusion.[2]

Strether's homely analysis, complete with its Emily Dickinson-like metaphysical conceit and domestic metaphor—that is, the comparison of diminished freedom and consciousness to a gourmet cook's template-form—is a remarkable conceptual stance in an age-old debate. Strether in effect condenses and names the position James himself exhibits throughout the novel as a whole, one that mediates equally between determinism and free agency. And that position in turn is identical to the one his brother William James expounded in his pragmatic philosophy. Regardless of the particular school of philosophy, however, Henry's supple engagement with this question is exceptional and impressive for a nonphilosopher.

A fourth reason for the novel's landmark esteem is that it is a perfect, consummately executed work of art at the level of structure and figurative language. For all its psychological authority, its internationalism, its restricted point of view, and its philosophical resonance, *The Ambassadors* is remarkably like a poem by Keats, Shakespeare, or Milton by dint of its intricate and interlocking systems of metaphorical leitmotif, emblematic episodes, repetition of structural pattern and bridgework, and parallelism amongst major and supporting characters. One sometimes overlooks this important feature of *The Ambassadors* for several reasons: first, because it is a long novel, neither a short lyric poem like a Keats ode nor a Shakespeare sonnet nor yet a work with the patently elevated subject of a verse epic; second, because many other issues—especially those addressing character motivation and cultural bias—bend our minds away from the kind of aesthetic imperatives that underlie its systems of structure and metaphor; third, because contemporary critical theory is now often inimical of formal excellence, even though at least one of its branches, that of deconstruction, is preoccupied with language and signification (though with its problematic nature rather then with its intact structures). Nevertheless, any real understanding of and appreciation for James's accomplishment requires an extensive examination and appreciation of this feature, the very one James himself seemed to value the most. For example, we can guess about the sheer extent to which James felt the germ permeate organically throughout *The Ambassadors,* since, as he said, the work composed itself "from the germ up" and then, as published, "fits again into its germ."[3]

James constructs, that is to say, Lambert Strether's compressed life history, up to his Howells-like lament in the garden (the melancholy utterance occurs almost halfway through the novel in Book Fifth), and then explores the consequences of the germ speech for the remainder of the narrative. What the composition and genesis of this book tell us is that, at every stage of the way and even afterward, James felt that his novel expanded from iterative versions of the same germ.[4] Hence it is crystal clear that he judged *The Ambassadors* his finest book precisely because of its special relation to that germ. By using the germ so effectively, he fused the new program of psychological realism with the demanding aesthetic tenets of earlier Coleridgean organic unity, something no one else in American fiction at that juncture in literary history had ever done.

A last major reason for the abiding importance of *The Ambassadors* is that all its artistry and complexity encases a deep structure or archetype of the fairy tale. Strether, like the primordial knight, is sent on a quest by his monarch and patron, Mrs. Abel Newsome. If he performs his appointed task, that of bringing back to her a prodigal son from the snares of the evil temptress Marie de Vionnet, Strether will be rewarded with her hand in marriage. While composing out of this structure, however, James has wrought brilliant reversals upon it: the hero is not young but a widower well into middle age; his damsel-monarch is both a rich bourgeois widow and "just a *moral* swell" (I, 67). Most important, Strether does not merely fail in his ambassadorial mission, he actually reverses his stance and seeks to prevent it, causing the other "ambassadors" to come from Woollett and discredit him! James's novel hereby begins to exemplify R. P. Blackmur's wonderful thesis, in "The Loose and Baggy Monsters of Henry James," that his complex idiom and elaboration are actually superimposed on a strict classical foundation.[5]

This final point relates to the late James's almost magical ability to take a relatively simple situation from everyday life and, by investing it with unforeseen complexity and nuance (simulated with the late prose style), ultimately convey a world replete with bewilderment and epistemological provisionalness—a sort of "subjunctive" reality, although one still tied, by a thread, to mimesis. Other enduring features of *The Ambassadors* not discussed in this brief chapter, such as its ambiguity or its status in between comedy and tragedy, are all connected to this last feature. While composing an artistic tour de force, James first forms it out of the deep archetype of the fable or fairy tale. Then he proceeds to erect atop this structural foundation a tragicomic American realistic novel of human bewilderment. That is quite a potpourri of major elements for a book that remains so unified.

3

Critical Reception

"Reception theory" is essentially the view that the history of any major work's reception may be justly thought of as the continuous accumulating meaning of that particular work. In the case of *The Ambassadors,* however, the history of its reception seems to recapitulate the principal contours of James's reputation as a whole. Indeed, the response to *The Ambassadors* in the international community of scholars and critics from James's time to the present almost constitutes a mini-history of the evolution and morphology of twentieth-century literary criticism itself.

To begin with, James was in effect the first major reader-in-response when, in his preface to the New York Edition, he sought to explain why he felt, after rereading it, that *The Ambassadors* was his strongest book. In 1903, the novel appeared first in serial form in *The North American Review,* then was published in book form by Methuen in London and Harper in New York. By November of that year James had already twice revised first the serial and then the English text. Then six years later he revised far more substantially for the Scribner's, or the New York, Edition. *The Ambassadors* appeared there as volumes XXI and XXII, introduced by the celebrated preface. Unlike most novelists, then, James was profoundly involved from the beginning with shaping the subsequent ways in which his book should be read.

Much has been made of his extensive influence in this regard, especially these days by some critics who feel compelled to deconstruct—that is, skeptically analyze—James's arguments in the New York prefaces regarding his sources or origins. To be sure, it is almost impossible to overstate his past influence, especially within the American academy. And yet even from the start reviewers tended often to divide into those who admired James's authority, subtlety, and discernment and others who deplored his obscure style, indefiniteness, and so-called effeminacy.[1]

We have already examined Ezra Pound's and T. S. Eliot's important advocations for establishing James with literary modernism. In general, James's early critics were writers themselves: Howells, Conrad, Ford Madox Ford, H. G. Wells, Rebecca West, Virginia Woolf, and Mrs. Humphrey Ward, the last of whom admired "the deep droughts from human life that [his work] represents ... [for] there is scarcely anything in human feeling, normal or strange, that he cannot describe or suggest."[2] T. S. Eliot's tribute includes his famous pronouncement that James "had a mind so fine that no idea could violate it," a locution some anti-Jamesians welcomed as hostile criticism. They were unaware from the context that Eliot is praising James—even singling him out among English and French writers—for never riding herd on an idea-ridden thesis but instead allowing his fiction to convey the malleability of experience. Hence, for Eliot, "James's critical genius comes out most tellingly in his mastery of, his baffling escape from, Ideas; a mastery and an escape which are perhaps the last test of a superior intelligence."[3]

The other major strand of early criticism stemmed in 1918 from Joseph Warren Beach and in 1921 from Percy Lubbock, both of whom made immensely important contributions to the reputation of *The Ambassadors.* Beach and Lubbock set the tone for academic, or "Jamesian," criticism by attending to theme and technique and by exhibiting respect for the New York prefaces, thereby establishing a pattern that dominated scholarship and classroom alike for well over half a century. The titles of Beach's and Lubbock's works alone, *The Method of Henry James* and *The Craft of Fiction,* bespeak serious preoccupation with Jamesian technique. Additionally, each followed James's lead in highlighting *The Ambassadors.* For Beach,

> the *ideal* of James is clearly a combination, or rather a *fusion,* of good taste with spiritual discernment, and perhaps the most complete, if not the most dramatic, instance of this fusion is ... Lambert Strether. For him there seems to be no such distinction between esthetic and ethic as perplexes us mortals.[4]

Lubbock goes at least as far by asserting Strether's mind to be so "fully dramatized" that the "art of dramatizing the picture of somebody's [inner] experience ... touches its limits. There is indeed no further for it to go."[5] *The Craft of Fiction* canonizes both James and *The Ambassadors* at the same time by applying tenets gleaned from James's prefaces and evaluating such classic writers as Tolstoy and Flaubert by "James" standards. Sometimes more Jamesian than James, Lubbock's book, along with Beach's, codified point of view and the dramatic method in fiction and set the stage for continued formal analysis on James for many decades to come. In short, the history of literary formalism—the study of form and technique as the gateway to meaning—and the history of *The Ambassadors* are one and the same. James became ensconced as "the Master," shaping the destiny of his own literary history, extending his dominion. This conception of Henry James as master remained unchallenged until the 1980s.

Negative judgment of James's work, brief as it was, occurred mostly in the 1920s, when it became fashionable to disfavor pre–World War I work. Although Hemingway and Gertrude Stein themselves much admired James, to others these writers' sparer idiom made James's late expressionistic style seem cumbersome and excessive. The stream-of-consciousness method, first named and explained by James's brother William in *The Principles of Psychology* (1890), was, as practiced by the modernists, intentionally more messy and wasteful than in James. For he sought not to *transcribe* the stream of thought but to *dramatize* it, largely through metaphor and adapted soliloquy. Actually James comes far closer to William's exposition of the concept than do the modernists who coined the expression for a literary method.

Into this milieu came Van Wyck Brooks's nationalistic critique of James as a failed American aesthete whose deracinating pilgrimage abroad resulted in late novels for which only "formal significance" counts and which otherwise are "exhalations of intellectual vapor."[6] Vernon Louis Parrington's influential Marxist literary history likewise deprecates James's "inner world of questioning and probing" and claims that even in his "subtle psychological enquiries he remained shut up within his own skull pan."[7]

The same climate produced E. M. Forster's 1927 objection to *The Ambassadors,* that the novel's "hourglass" symmetry is an exquisite pattern but at the "enormous sacrifice" of "human life," since the book is peopled by characters with huge heads and tiny legs.[8] Several decades after this brief period of anti-Jamesianism, in 1962, Maxwell Geismar tried one last time, in *Henry James and the Jacobites,* to mount a frontal attack on him and the literary academy.[9] Geismar's assault is essentially a more sarcastic reconstruction of the argument previously made by Van Wyck Brooks, to whom he dedicated the book. But by 1962 Geismar's thesis served only to clarify James's permanence at the top of the genre, for although Geismar was often discussed in the classroom, his book retarded the great proliferation of "Jacobite," or pro-Jamesian, scholarship and criticism not one iota.

What had already begun after the period of Brooks, Parrington, and Forster's criticism was a swift resurgence of work on James by Cornelia Kelley, Constance Rourke, and many others. Blackmur's *Art of the Novel* (1934) first collected the New York prefaces between the covers of one book and introduced them brilliantly by isolating and, in a fluid way, codifying James's literary tenets. Blackmur thereby extended the tradition of Beach and Lubbock.[10] That same year there appeared a special issue of *Hound and Horn,* "Homage to Henry James," edited by Yvor Winters and Allen Tate, which contained 13 essays by such notables as Marianne Moore and Edmund Wilson. The issue opened the way for an unstinting flood of criticism that swamped Geismar in the early 60s and continues to this day.[11]

Whereas Graham Greene ranked James with Shakespeare in his "sense of evil, religious in its intensity," F. O. Matthiessen's aesthetic-moral approach in *Henry James: The Major Phase* (1944) stressed character, theme, metaphor, and structure in *The Ambassadors*.[12] Unlike Yvor Winters and others who focused primarily on Strether as evolving the New England conscience beyond its early Calvinist and Unitarian phases, Matthiessen shifted the novel's center of gravity to Madame de Vionnet's attraction and presence as "a living tap root" to the past, an "exquisite product of tradition," and a person whose suffering equals Strether's.[13]

The 1950s and 1960s witnessed a spate of James studies, including the emergence of Leon Edel's five-volume masterpiece of Freudian biography, *The Life of Henry James,* which stressed the personal, passional roots of characters like Strether. Such critics as Sallie Sears and J. A. Ward strove to elaborate the "darker" James expostulated earlier by Stephen Spender and Graham Greene.[14] But the most quietly important study of the period was possibly Christof Wegelin's *The Image of Europe in Henry James,* 1958. This deceptively slim volume explored the complexities in James of the international theme everyone had been talking, teaching, and writing about but had never put together with quite the right emphasis on James's "middle" viewpoint in probing nationalist provincialism on all sides. Moreover, Wegelin cites Strether's special educative process and emphasizes his pragmatic openness of mind.[15]

The most stunning discussion of all during this period was Ian Watt's long and powerful explication in 1960 of the first paragraph of *The Ambassadors,* an amazing critical performance that not only verified James's high artistic program but recognized his ties with poetry. Watt concludes that

> The most obvious and demonstrable features of James's prose style, its vocabulary and syntax, are direct reflections of his attitude to life and his conception of the novel; and these features, like the relation of the paragraph to the rest of the novel, and to other novels, make clear that the notorious idiosyncrasies of Jamesian prose are directly related to the imperatives which led

him to develop a narrative texture as richly complicated and as highly organized as that of poetry.[16]

The 1970s, 1980s, and 1990s have been periods of downright centrifugal academic discussion on James. The number of book-length studies alone has been tremendous, and only a few may be culled and cited. In 1976, Ruth B. Yeazell addressed once more the richness of metaphor and syntax of James's late style in criticism that extended Ian Watt's thesis to all the major late novels and built on the fine compilation of James's figurative language a decade earlier by Robert Gale.[17] Also, Sergio Perosa in *Henry James and the Experimental Novel* (1978) anticipated brilliantly the shift in James studies the following decade by designating him "a great-uncle of postmodernism."[18]

Meanwhile reader-response studies of James began appearing more and more frequently in the journals. In hindsight it is now clear that reader-response criticism—the view that a text like *The Ambassadors* comes to life in the reader—was anticipated as early as Lubbock and even James himself in the New York prefaces. In 1979, however, Nicola Bradbury composed what is still the best reader-response interpretation of the major-phase fiction. Her *Henry James: The Later Novels* shows parallelism between the characters' attempts at perception, the author's at expression, and the readers' at understanding. In Bradbury's deft analysis of *The Ambassadors,* Strether achieves negative capability like T. S. Eliot's "still point," in which he vanishes with the exposure of "Chad's baseness" at deserting Madame de Vionnet to become indissolubly fused with the "the narrator."[19] Although it is not necessary to accept Bradbury's specific reading, *The Ambassadors* will always be "a natural" for reader-response criticism, since the novel places the reader inside Strether's unfolding process of bewilderment and discovery—what James in the preface calls "his very gropings."[20]

Beginning in the 1980s, Henry James's criticism has been shifting significantly enough to constitute a "second wave," as I have elsewhere argued.[21] This second wave may be likened to the "second wind" Strether feels in *The Ambassadors,* when he experiences in Gloriani's garden on the Left Bank of Paris a "sweeping away, as by a last brush, [of] his usual landmarks and terms" (I, 195). In the case of

James's criticism, the "usual landmarks"—that is, the "first wave"—constituted his dominion extending onward from Lubbock's *Craft of Fiction* through Wayne C. Booth's *Rhetoric of Fiction,* signifying the marriage of formal analysis and reader response.[22] The reason this second wave has occurred is that James has now become a receptacle for all the divergent strands of postmodern critical theory, as distinct from the literary criticism that originally made his reputation during the "first wave." It is unusual that James has become the darling of the academy, so to speak, on the sometimes opposing critical and ideological grounds from those that made him revered earlier.

Although Sarah Daugherty and Daniel M. Fogel both wrote excellent traditional studies of James in 1981, the second with its fine reading of *The Ambassadors* executing the dialectic of spiral return found in the great Romantic poetry,[23] by 1984 James was already a force in postmodern criticism. That same year John Carlos Rowe published *The Theoretical Dimensions of Henry James,* a book that Nicola Bradbury has called "a kind of *summa* in which each chapter tests a major contemporary theory in application to James's work."[24] Using James's fiction like a refracting prism for the shaft of contemporary theory, Rowe eventually aligns himself with what he calls "Deconstruction in America."[25]

As influential as he swiftly became, Rowe was by no means the only major new-wave James critic. Also in 1984 Mark Seltzer lauded James as an artistic power figure and Elizabeth Allen and Virginia Fowler praised him as a feminist.[26] During the same time frame, from 1983 to 1986, James the heretofore monastic writer turned into a hardworking professional concerned with market and popularity thanks to studies by Marcia Jacobson, Anne T. Margolis, and Michael Anesko, who proposed that his "friction with the market" (James's own phrase) was even productive of his artistic independence.[27] Moreover, in 1986 Donna Przybylowicz, in *Desire and Repression,* extended Leon Edel's neo-Freudianism to Jacques Lacan's revisionist psychoanalytic theory. Since then such other critics as William Veeder and Beth Sharon Ash have likewise applied post-Freudian psychoanalysis to James's fiction.[28]

Almost as though it were simulating John Carlos Rowe's succession of different critical schools, James criticism has continued to diversify. Paul Armstrong's study of James's modernism, *The Challenge of Bewilderment,* appeared in 1987. It features a brilliant discussion of *The Ambassadors,* concerning in particular Lambert Strether's problem-laden powers of "construal," his "bridge over the darkness [by] the ceaseless meaning-making of [his] consciousness."[29] We shall see in more detail in chapter 5 how Armstrong exhibits Strether's system of "hermeneutics"—his system of interpretation—within a world and reality of constant flux.

More new critical waves have come ashore, so to speak. In 1989 feminist and historian Alfred Habegger, in *Henry James and the 'Woman Business,'* was already disputing Allen and Fowler's prowoman readings, claiming instead that James in his fiction appropriates his father's reactionary and repressive views on women and marriage.[30] That same year David McWhirter sought to bring back close reading of the three major-phase novels while expounding a series of thematic antimonies resolved only in *The Golden Bowl.* McWhirter is unusual in that he extensively criticizes *The Ambassadors,* Strether, and James himself for succumbing to the "figuration of desire" and thereby falling short of expressing genuine love.[31]

Throughout the period of 1986 to 1993, Adeline Tintner established herself without peer in tracing James's vast miscellany of iconographical, literary, and popular sources and analogues. Originally a student and colleague of Leon Edel's, Tintner ever since the 1940s had in a sense buffeted the critical winds of theoretical criticism and persisted in "old-time" (but also quite creative) source-analogue approaches. A genius for discovering the novelist's transmuted sources, Tintner also collaborated with Edel on *The Library of Henry James* (1987), a valuable resource and research tool supportive of the sort of criticism she herself practices well.[32]

Daniel M. Fogel returned with *Covert Relations* (1990), which demonstrates James's anxiety-provoking influence upon Joyce and Woolf, an approach rather different from his Romantic-structure thesis of 1981. Fogel unearths patterns of influence from *The Ambassadors* and *Portrait of the Artist, Ulysses, Mrs. Dalloway,* and Woolf's "Phases of Fiction." Indeed, James's masterpiece constitutes, says Fogel, "[t]he Narrow Bridge of Art" to the modern novel.[33] The same

year, Philip Horne's *Henry James and Revision,* although it acknowledges the work on James's professionalism by Michael Anesko et al.,
demonstrates anew the meticulous artistry of his revisions and thereby
implicitly reestablishes authority for the New York prefaces.[34]

The nineties is an era for culture studies, and James has his share
with important work by Ross Posnock and Susan Griffin (the present
editor of *The Henry James Review* and successor of Daniel M. Fogel,
its founder in 1979). Griffin's *Historical Eye: The Texture of the Visual
in Late James* extends such interdisciplinary approaches as Tintner's in
order to correlate the triad of James's visual imagination, American-
art criticism of the same period, and the functionalist psychology of
William James. In her reading of *The Ambassadors,* Lambert Strether
embodies as no one else William James's theory of perception—as we
shall see later in chapter 6. Ross Posnock, in *The Trial of Curiosity,*
claims to "tak[e] Henry James seriously as an intellectual," that is, as
someone who "critically examines contemporary cultural, social, and
political issues."[35] Posnock's own mentors in this enterprise include
such cultural theorists as Walter Benjamin, Richard Rorty, and especially Theodor Adorno. Posnock's "Henry James" is now regarded as a
forerunner of the "politics of non-identity" assumed and practiced by
today's "cultural materialists"—that is, Marxist critics who generally
hold that literature is socially constructed.

Other branches of second-wave criticism continue apace to this
day. Priscilla Walton, Mary Cross, and Paul Beidler continue to work
with French theory. Beidler, for instance, applies Jacques Derrida's
study of the "parergon," or supplemental frame, to *The Ambassadors*
and even to the "parergonal nature" of the hero Strether, who must
free himself from Paris in order to discover the framing place in his
own life. Similarly, Julie Rivkin reads *The Ambassadors* as a model of
Derrida's theories of "supplemental meaning," that is, the deferral or
postponement of any final determinate meaning in the wake of the in-
stability of all language.[36]

Different kinds of cultural criticism carry on in James. Kelly
Cannon's gender study of the novelist contends that Strether in particular fails to meet his contemporary stereotype of masculinity, yet he
has a certain added freedom at the margins of society. And in *Black*

and White Strangers, Kenneth Warren proposes that such late-nineteenth-century realists as James actually exacerbated problems of race they would have liked to ameliorate. For instance, Strether's attack in *The Ambassadors* on "Northern femininity" by his rejection of Mrs. Newsome undermines the "New England tradition of feminist reform" that liberal and progressive voices needed to support during such a crucial period in American racial history.[37] Finally, Carol Holly's recent book *Intensely Family* is a cultural biography that investigates the complex relationship of inherited family shame with James's late autobiographies; she extends and embodies Paul John Eakin's theories regarding the transactions and differences between biography and autobiography.[38]

When we look back over the last several decades, one of the richest veins of discussion has been that of James and philosophy. It more or less began with my *Henry James and Pragmatistic Thought* in 1974, the first comprehensive examination of the profound connections between the novelist's late work and his philosopher brother's thought; in that work I challenged the prevailing views of opposition that F. O. Mathiessen and Ralph Barton Perry held at that time. Four years later Stephen Donadio unearthed a creative parallel between James and Nietzsche and sought to redefine Jamesian perception as an act of will. Then in 1983 Paul Armstrong penned an illuminating analysis, *The Phenomenology of Henry James,* that relates James's fiction to the one twentieth-century philosophical school that parallels his work more than any other. Finally, in 1993, 10 years after Paul Armstrong's study and some 20 years after mine, Merle Williams wrote *Henry James and the Philosophical Novel.* This study rigorously blends phenomenology—the investigation of appearances as apprehended by consciousness (a school whose origins lie in William James)—with Jacques Derrida's skeptical viewpoint.[39]

When we survey James's philosophical criticism over this 20-year period, then, we find contours similar to James literary criticism as a whole, with traditional arguments that debate, but are also mediated by, postmodern or revisionist theory. And we likewise find that *The Ambassadors* and Strether inevitably constitute a focal point, as has been the case with James criticism generally.[40]

What should the student of James make of this complex critical history in which resides an equally complex novel? Is a book with the credentials of *The Ambassadors* too formidable? Is the student better off with James's contemporary Mark Twain, whose broad humor and sarcastic denunciation seem more accessible? Even a number of sophisticated New Yorkers, it is now said, have taken up Leon Edel's vivid biography rather than its subject, and others have become devourers of the newly edited correspondence between William and Henry rather than taking on the challenges of the philosopher or the novelist firsthand.[41]

Yet for all this assumed intimidation, the student reading *The Ambassadors* has a unique opportunity to enter with Lambert Strether into a veritable diplomatic "mine field," alongside a male character who has most of the best traits of both genders. The student also has an opportunity to piece together gradually, as with the Byzantium mosaics celebrated by Yeats, all the poetic elements that converge into the high artistry of this book. The same student discovers the extent to which James, largely through his minute rendering of consciousness, brings surprising drama to the most everyday and mundane experiences; yet it's also possible to see how such a quotidian drama of consciousness opens up new areas of bewilderment as the price of discovery. Indeed, the ironic relationship between new discovery and new bewilderment governs *The Ambassadors* from beginning to end, as we shall see presently.

The history of the book's reception, coterminous with the history of James criticism and of modern criticism itself, surely must tell us that *The Ambassadors* is, as James once said, "a living thing, all one and continuous, like any other organism."[42] Clearly such vitality is at least as important as is the presence of complexity in the history of the novel's reception. Admittedly, Ross Posnock sounds the contemporary note of the confident "second wave" critic when he proposes that we "dismantl[e] the inert, enshrined formalist Henry James that was erected in the 1950s." Yet for today's students, who already hear quite a bit on campuses about the "patriarchy and classical masculinity" that Posnock further claims James will "puncture" if we just "set [him] aside" as "this sacred icon"[43]—for these students there may actually be as much newness and excitement in learning how to catch on to the cadences in his late style as there is in catching on to his ideological rhythms in cadence with his political correctness. Fusing the first and second waves in the classroom, so to speak, is perhaps not impossible. But surely the student must first comprehend, and not just in some token way, the experience of which Philip Fisher writes:

> One of the master texts of a whole generation of American study was Henry James's *The Ambassadors,* perhaps from an academic point of view the most perfect text written by an American. James's hero Strether creates a myth of Paris, a myth of his charge, Chad, a myth of Chad's relation to Mme. de Vionnet. Each myth is betrayed by fact, stained by the complexity of the real world. An entire academic generation saw its own love of criticism, observation, nuance, disappointment, myth and defeat in James's novel.[44]

This experience may not be as nostalgic as Fisher intends. More than a quarter of a century ago, I invariably found my own students struggling at first to understand and appreciate the later James, though a certain number of them tended eventually to respond given enough time. Recently, however, one of my finest students, who was attending my seminar on James's fiction and postmodern criticism, informed me that she "loved" reading *The Ambassadors* and thought the prose beautiful and accessible given some guidance. But she also found most of the contemporary criticism and theory we were reading about James's novels absolutely "impenetrable" and "hopelessly removed from James," even though all the political issues themselves were, she said, as familiar to her as the "student life programs" on our campus. After speaking with her, I ruminated for some time (like Strether) about the momentous change in the past 25-plus years that has enabled undergraduates with some guidance to comprehend and enjoy the text of a late-James novel more swiftly than in the past. Only gradually did I begin to attend to the other half of her revelation—the part regarding postmodern criticism. The chapters that follow, although explicitly indebted to contemporary James critics, as will be seen, attempt mostly to showcase the sort of novel my student said she loved.[45]

A READING

4

James's Narrative System: Point of View and Consciousness

Despite the novel's celebrated complexity, what occurs "externally" in *The Ambassadors* can seem reasonably simple, though hardly simplistic. A genteel but poor 55-year-old New Englander, Louis Lambert Strether, is sent as ambassador by a rich widow, Mrs. Abel Newsome, with whom Strether has an understanding of betrothal, to rescue her son Chad from an unsavory Parisian woman and return the young man to work at the family's manufacturing business in Woollett, Massachusetts. Once in Paris, however, Strether responds to his own dormant memories of youth in Paris: he regrets that he has failed "to live," he admires and respects the allegedly "venal" woman, Marie de Vionnet (in age almost halfway between Chad and himself), he begins to succumb to Chad's "transformation" under her influence as an improvement, and he ends up reversing his entire stance. Now he becomes the ambassador *for* Chad's relationship with Madame de Vionnet and in that process gradually loses everything—Mrs. Newsome's financial support and of course her withdrawn hand in marriage. By chance discovery he even loses in dramatic fashion his heretofore elevated view of Chad and Marie's platonic relationship. These various

ironic reversals are matched and compounded by Chad's simultaneously changing his mind about Marie and, despite Strether's valiant
pleas, choosing to abandon her and return home to pursue the new
"art of advertisement" for the Woollett family business. So even as he
becomes dispossessed, so to speak, Strether must reevaluate everything he recently has come to embrace and believe in: his own declaration "to live" together with the authenticity of Chad's transformation
and hence the ultimate reality of the "improvement" wrought by
Marie de Vionnet—with whom Strether himself has all but fallen in
love.

One senses immediately that James's external plot has a certain
classical symmetry and irony reminiscent of Aristotle's tenets in the
Poetics. In fact, however, James inverts Aristotle by making his narrative character driven rather than event driven. Even so, by allowing
character to determine incident James does end up with his own classical equivalence and parallel, his "obverse" to Aristotle, as it were. He
accomplishes this feat by subordinating everything else to Strether
alone and by confining the reader's process of discovery to that of
Strether's. As mentioned already, *The Ambassadors* is regarded as a triumph of the Jamesian restricted point of view: we learn pretty much
only as stimuli impinge on Strether, register in his consciousness, and
are thereby relayed to us as we read.[1]

One of the very first people to focus on this achievement was
James himself. He tells us in the New York Edition preface that "every
question of form ... paled in the light of the major propriety ... that
of employing but one centre and keeping it all within my hero's compass." He further explains:

> Other persons in no small number were to people the scene, and
> each with his or her axe to grind, his or her situation to treat....
> But Strether's sense of these things, and Strether's only, should
> avail me for showing them; I should know them but through his
> more or less groping knowledge of them, since his very gropings
> would figure among his most interesting motions [by] giv[ing] me
> more of the effect I should be most "after" than all other possible
> observances together.[2]

The story of *The Ambassadors,* then, is that all the crucial external events are subordinated to Strether's interior perception and analysis of them, which ultimately engenders his volte-face, his change of mind and heart regarding his mission. An entire generation of students and teachers might be said to have learned about the technique of narrative point of view by using *The Ambassadors* to evaluate the achievement of other authors, often under the guidance of James's literary executor, Percy Lubbock, in his book *The Craft of Fiction.* Nowadays, to be sure, those who concern themselves with Jamesian point of view may wish just as often to consider the ingenious ways James escapes from the limitations of his confining point of view to expand the horizons of the novel's universe. Most frequently he does it by layering the *narrative* consciousness over that of the *character's* point of view in ways that the two mutually interact. In any case, the fact is that most college students, as yet intrinsically free from the anxieties of postmodern criticism, remain fascinated by the classic technique: the way James "stays within" Strether, or the way he still "gets beyond" Strether, either by "intruding" from time to time or, more pervasively, by subtly insinuating additional elements that shape the reader's response.

In traditional terms, then, the point-of-view issue is one of the main ingredients for comprehending and appreciating in this novel James's "large unity," as he himself enunciated it in the same preface.[3] Not surprisingly, however, the general decline of interest in point of view among postmodern critics is directly proportional to these same critics' fierce suspicion of the concept of artistic unity, which they sometimes regard as a formalist disguise for political repression, psychoanalytic drives, or even some combination of gender, racial, or class bias. But again, fresh students of James, unlike their betters, still seem to care about unity and hence about James's narrative point of view. In any event, *The Ambassadors* remains an exemplary text for addressing and assessing these issues in James. This would be so even if one were to don the au courant position (which I tend not very often to do in this study) that this novel, like that by any major author, is ultimately a nexus of literature, culture, and semiotics.

In examining James's restricted narrative method, it is sometimes helpful to learn at least a few of his critical terms, most of which are scattered throughout the New York prefaces, his notebooks, and various critical essays. For example, he likes to call his central-viewpoint character his "register" or his "deputy." This is of course Strether's quintessential role in *The Ambassadors*. Still another expression, "central intelligence"—which James sometimes calls simply "intelligence"—is a term critics frequently use to designate viewpoint characters like Strether, but in fact James means something different by it; by "central intelligence" he means the organizing, unifying *narrative* consciousness, the "voice," if you will, unless the work happens to be rendered through first-person narration. James greatly preferred not to use first-person narration in his novels, although he makes very successful use of it in his tales along with third-person presentation. Indeed, he specifically rejected the first-person method in his preface to *The Ambassadors* as unsuitable for his purpose, warning that if he had made Strether "at once hero and historian, endowed him with the romantic privilege of the 'first person,' " his novel would have betrayed "the darkest abyss of romance" and would have forced him to "smuggle" all sorts of "queer matters ... in by a back door."[4] Instead, he is gratified that Strether is "encaged and provided for" so as to forestall "the terrible *fluidity* of self-revelation."[5]

What James is getting at here is the advantage of having a third-person narrative voice shape the dramatic illusion of reality emanating from Strether's consciousness and, at the same time, allow for greater natural expansiveness than is possible with first-person. To put it another way, James employs an unnamed narrator who is not an actor in the story yet does not possess the traditional omniscience of the storyteller. His narrator (presumably an aspect of James himself) is, compared to an omniscient storyteller, about as proportionately restricted in his knowledge as is the viewpoint character to the selfsame narrator. What James gains by this is a system that is 1) very flexible, thanks to the openness and range of third-person narration; 2) dramatically restricted, thanks to the epistemological limits of the viewpoint character; and 3) very plausible and realistic, thanks to the graded, respective limitations of both narrator and viewpoint deputy.

Such special layering of narrator and deputy makes it doubly important that we not misunderstand a concept like "central intelligence": the "intelligence" is what allows James to *both* merge with and "get beyond" Strether in a flexible, restricted narratology. I should point out as well that, although James never mentions it, his objections in the preface to first-person narration clearly arise from his dissatisfaction with *The Sacred Fount* (1901), the first-person novel he composed just before *The Ambassadors* and even overlapped with it. *The Sacred Fount*'s experimental nature has made it newly attractive to some branches of contemporary theory, to be sure, but the novel has always been plagued by its irreducible ambiguity, which results in great part from its lack of a clarifying narrator, or "central intelligence." James did not include the work in the New York Edition. On the other hand, *The Turn of the Screw* (1898), written just a couple of years earlier, does employ first-person narration with great success and is perhaps most celebrated *for* its ambiguity in the wake of the governess's claims. Clearly, for James, the first-person system worked better with the tale than with the novel, and he knew it. For that matter, the famous governess could even be said to exhibit "the terrible *fluidity* of self-revelation." Hence what is wrong with a technique in one case becomes in another case what is right in portraying a disturbed character.

Two other critical terms from James's criticism—besides "germ" and "ficelle," which are discussed in earlier chapters—need to be learned as helpful for any examination of *The Ambassadors*. "Picture" and "scene"—so named by James—refer to his two principal structural elements, especially in the late novels. "Picture" designates specifically the rendering of interior thought, such as Strether's or that of any other deputy. "Scene" refers to the characters in action, speech, and dialogue. In first attempting to explain James's system, Percy Lubbock used the expressions "the panoramic" and "the dramatic."[6] Lubbock's substitute terms are propitious insofar as they distinguish the more ranging nature of "picture" from the confined, stagelike nature of scene. But they greatly mislead from another standpoint. In James, picture is always extremely dramatic, as evidenced by Strether's two great meditations in Books Second and Eleventh, as well as by other episodes, such as his first reaction to the silent, physical presence of Chad in Book Third. Scene is of course also, and in a sense more obviously, dramatic, since in *The Ambassadors* scenes comprise Strether's many conversations with all the principal supporting figures—ficelles or otherwise: Waymarsh, little Bilham, Chad, Sarah Pocock, Marie de Vionnet, Maria Gostrey (but not Mrs. Newsome, who never appears and is made present through picture or else in scenic conversation with others).

The great point about the picture-and-scene system in Henry James is that the two elements alternate and complement one another with great elasticity. The typical chapter in *The Ambassadors* begins with several paragraphs of picture and then modulates into scene. Less frequently but just as effective, James occasionally begins a chapter with a bit of scene and then allows it to rise to ruminating picture triggered by the scene's content. In *The Ambassadors* what is distinctive is that Strether takes part in every dialogue, but in picture he then interprets to himself what his interlocutors say, how they say it, and what the implications might be. That James uses and blends the dramatic intensity of *both* picture and scene rather than one technique or the other by itself makes for a far more unified system, like a living alternating polarity rather than two different techniques merely "taking turns." In many ways the picture-and-scene approach is the structural triumph of the late James.

The technique came about after James was hissed from the legitimate stage. In effect, he took his playwriting mode and gradually married it to the rendering of interior consciousness. During the experimental period preceding *The Ambassadors,* he first wrote one novel, *The Awkward Age* (1899), using only the scenic system. Then he wrote another, *What Maisie Knew* (1897), attempting to confine himself to the picture system. In still another, *The Spoils of Poynton* (1897), he composed the early chapters in picture and the later ones mostly in scene. But when he came to write *The Ambassadors,* he skillfully modulated the two back and forth from beginning to end.[7] Essentially, the effect is at least as musical as it is more obviously visual.

Although James's critical terms surely meant a great deal to him—helping him not only to explain his work but also, as his *Note-*

books makes clear, to write it—they can seem confusing at times to the reader or student. For example, when James is not referring to a "register" or "deputy," he is likely to allude to Strether as his "center," by which he means his imputed center of consciousness in the novel. In such instances, therefore, he does *not* mean his "central intelligence," or the narrative consciousness. Such potential confusion makes it understandable that some critics and teachers call the viewpoint character James's "central intelligence," although such a determination is wrong and in fact obscures some of the best elements of James's narration. The fiction of his early and middle periods, before *The Ambassadors,* shows a variety of narratology, from the use of the omniscient narrator and letter writers to first-person and autobiographical narrators. All of his methods, however, tended from early on in his career to allow his fictional situations to convey "the impression of life," by reducing as much as possible purely authorial commentary. Moreover, when he does use such commentary, as in *The Portrait of a Lady,* for instance, he never abandons the provisional nature of human and social relationships, which invariably is his core subject. For example, at the conclusion of *The Portrait,* Isabel Archer, the heroine, experiences hard-burning suitor Casper Goodwood's frustration, aggression, and assault as he is about to kiss her passionately. "[Casper] had suddenly given up argument," the narrator informs us, "and his voice seemed to come, harsh and terrible, through a confusion of vaguer sounds."

This is what Isabel feels, and appropriately so, since Casper is about to grab her and kiss her "like white lightning." And yet the narrator at just this moment chooses to "intrude" with the following comment: "This, however, of course, was but a subjective fact, as the metaphysicians say; the confusion, the noise of waters, all the rest of it, were in her own swimming head."[8] Although James wrote *The Portrait of a Lady* 20 years before *The Ambassadors,* the third-person narrator in *The Portrait* already functions to convey the deeper enigma of interpersonal relations. James's narrators, it can be said, even when technically omniscient always reinforce the open-ended provisionalness of life's meaning.

Something like a distinction between merely technical omniscience and a truly substantive omniscience, as in Fielding, Thackeray,

Dickens, and others, may clarify James's strong criticism of Anthony Trollope in "The Art of Fiction" (1884). Although Trollope is an author whose subject matter—mundane and subtle personal and social relations—shares much with James himself,[9] the novelist objects to Trollope's "habit of giving [himself] away which must often bring tears to the eyes of people who take their fiction seriously." James goes on to clarify his point:

> In a digression, a paragraph or an aside, [Trollope] concedes to the reader that he and this trusting friend are only "making believe." He admits that the events he narrates have not really happened, and that he can give his narrative any turn the reader may like best. Such a betrayal of a sacred office seems to me, I confess, a terrible crime; it is what I mean by the attitude of apology, and it shocks me every whit as much in Trollope as it would have shocked me in Gibbon or Macaulay. It implies that the novelist is less occupied in looking for the truth ... than the historian, and in doing so it deprives him at a stroke of all his standing room.[10]

James's "central intelligence," whether in *The Portrait of a Lady* or later in *The Ambassadors,* is a far cry from the authorial voice in Trollope. His narrative consciousness does not wish to sever "the illusion of life," which James believes is really the telos of fiction. For him, as for George Eliot, the novel imparts probable truths about human relationships as seriously and conscientiously as does the historian in his or her pursuit of findings in documents and anthropology.

In putting together his fictional system of indirection in *The Ambassadors,* James makes Lambert Strether both the observer of and participant in the action as it happens. All the information about previous occurrences elsewhere either comes to us through his memory and intuition or reaches him through dialogue. But the narrating voice remains in the third person. This voice may assume an authorial tenor when, for instance, intervals of time are passed over. But there is no attempt to balance Strether's point of view against that of any of the other figures. Most important, James does not "go behind" any other character to dramatize an alternative consciousness.[11]

He does, however, as mentioned earlier, make extensive use of the ficelle. Ficelles are "the reader's friend" and "direct aid[s] to lucidity" by virtue of relieving the figure from whose point of view the story is told the tediousness of conveying everything the reader needs to know.[12] They also relieve the narrator in similar fashion. Ficelles like little Bilham, Waymarsh, or Maria Gostrey can also, however, function thematically as mirror images—or else opposites—in delineating the deeper elements of Strether's character. For example, little Bilham, the amiable young American artist, is a manifestation of Strether's own youth and simultaneously a spiritual kinsman and substitute for his lost son. Alternatively, Chad, who actually would be his stepson if Strether married Mrs. Newsome, is never compatible with Strether in temperament, compassion, imagination, or purpose. Waymarsh, who finds Europe so profoundly uncomfortable that it triggers within him a "sacred rage" against it, is thereby a foil to Strether. At the beginning, Waymarsh is "dog tired" and wants to return home, whereas Strether was "dog tired" when he sailed but is now strangely rejuvenated. As for Maria Gostrey, his Europeanized American guide and confidant, she is worldly wise as opposed to Strether's uncertainty and bewilderment: she "gave [Strether] a sense of her easy movement through the maze he had but begun to tread." She is also a shrewd bargainer with a flat like a "brown pirate's cave" (I, 80), whereas Strether seems congenitally incapable of taking anything for himself from anybody. These ficelle figures, in short, reflect and illuminate emblematically as mirrors and prisms various aspects of Strether's character as well as the broader personal, social, and cultural ambience in which they all move.

The reader can best grasp the heart of James's narrative system—the dramatization of Strether's consciousness—by our looking at some exemplary instances of it. Of special importance is the way James allows his reader to collaborate with Strether's processes, whether of discovery or regret. A prime instance is Strether's meditation in the Luxembourg Gardens in Book Second, after he receives a missive from Mrs. Newsome that he should indulge in no activities that detract from his moral task at hand. Strether finds, alas, he has already reawakened to the city's stimulating presence, which in turn has the effect of triggering his sense of deep regret at the course of his life ever since first coming to Paris many years ago as a newly married young man.

James's narrator, in a most authorial mode, observes, "It will have been sufficiently seen that [Strether] was not a man to neglect any good chance for reflexion" (I, 89–90). This statement underscores the deep connection between Strether's character and James's method; however, it does not give us the shared experience between reader and Strether that the "reflexion" itself does. Strether's memories crowd him. He thinks of "the young wife he had early lost and the young son he had stupidly sacrificed," a youngster who "had died at school of rapid diphtheria" and might not have "if he had not in those years so insanely given himself to missing the mother."

> This was doubtless but the secret habit of sorrow, which had slowly given way to time; yet there remained an ache sharp enough to make the spirit, at the sight now and again of some fair young man just growing up, wince with the thought of an opportunity lost. Had ever a man, he had finally fallen into the way of asking himself, lost so much and even done so much for so little? (I, 84)

An enormous part of Strether's present sense of life failure is his newly released memory of the special pledge he made long ago when he was first exposed to the wonders of Paris. His regret from that memory continues to ramify in this example, also from Book Second, of the Jamesian picture method:

> The special spring that had constantly played for him the day before was the recognition—frequent enough to surprise him—of the promises to himself that he had after his other visit never kept. The reminiscence today most quickened for him was that of the vow taken in the course of the pilgrimage that, newly-married, with the War just over, and helplessly young in spite of it, he had recklessly made with the creature who was so much younger still. It had been ... this private pledge of his own to treat the occasion as a relation formed with the higher culture and see that, as they

said at Woollett, it should bear a good harvest. He had believed, sailing home again, that he had gained something great, and his theory—with an elaborate innocent plan of reading, digesting, coming back even, every few years—had then been to preserve, cherish and extend it. (I, 85–86)

In rueful contrast to these lovely expectations in the bloom of his youth is Strether's present realization that his occupation as editor of the modest *Woollett Review*—his "relation with the higher culture"—is undistinguished and, such as it is, paid for by Mrs. Newsome: "He was Lambert Strether because he was on the cover, whereas it should have been, for anything like glory, that he was on the cover because he was Lambert Strether" (I, 84).

As always with Strether, the interior exploration of all these issues eventually brings him back full circle to the James-like "germ" that first gives rise to it, the dictum from Mrs. Newsome regarding his conduct in light of his mission. Yet Strether cannot just put aside Paris's tantalizing power and manifold associations.

Was he to renounce all amusement for the sweet sake of that [deputized] authority? and *would* such renouncement give him for Chad a moral glamour? ... His greatest uneasiness seemed to peep at him out of the imminent impression that almost any acceptance of Paris might give one's authority away. It hung before him, this morning, the vast bright Babylon, like some hard iridescent object, a jewel brilliant and hard, in which parts were not to be discriminated nor differences comfortably marked. It twinkled and trembled and melted together, and what seemed all surface one moment seemed all depth the next. It was a place of which, unmistakably, Chad was fond; wherefore if he, Strether, should like it too much, what on earth, with such a bond, would become of either of them? (I, 89)

In this early meditation it is significant that Strether has yet to meet Chad, the focus of so much of his thought. After he gets up and leaves the Luxembourg Gardens, he walks back across the Seine to the Right Bank and the Boulevard Malesherbes, where Chad's flat is on the third floor. When he looks up, he sees a young man on the balcony whom he naturally expects to be Chad. But when he looks more closely, he discovers it is someone else. This young man, a close friend of Chad's named John Little Bilham, is to become Strether's closest male friend in the novel, the one to whom he will eventually deliver the germ speech (and who is thereby based on Jonathan Sturges, to whom Howells exclaimed, "Live all you can!").

James's narrative system is typically skillful and dense here. Strether's memories of high culture, his need to redeem the idealization of his youth, his wish for the return of the son he lost—all of these elements are fused in little Bilham. That is why James has Strether walk to meet him, so to speak, as the culmination of the chapter. That is also why Strether thinks he is about to meet Chad. Finally, that is why Strether's gaze is "elevated" to the third-floor balcony where little Bilham—not Chad—stands. The hallmark of James's narrative system is its virtuoso confluence of all these elements at once.

Moreover, the extended metaphor of Paris-as-jewel captures the very nexus of Strether's cognitive bewilderment; what seems "all surface" one moment seems "all depth" the next. This remarkable conceit—again, as so often with James, reminiscent of Emily Dickinson—manages to convey the "felt life" of James's deputy throughout the novel. As such, it denominates the sense of the world's reality mediated through Strether's consciousness throughout *The Ambassadors*. Finally, the same metaphor also corresponds to the epistemological doctrines of William James's pragmatic philosophy, but that is an issue to be examined later.

Another fine instance of James's point-of-view system can be found in Strether's captivated response to Chad when he actually does meet him, at the end of Book Third. Chad has purposefully stayed out of Strether's way for a week or so, thereby adroitly allowing for Strether's series of concatenating impressions—the young man's tasteful rooms in Malesherbes, the acquaintance with his young friends, especially little Bilham, whose "mention of [Chad] was of a kind to do him honour" (I, 117), and above all else "Europe" and "dear old Paris" itself (I, 134). In the wake of all this, Chad makes a calculated appearance by walking into a box at the Theatre de Comedie Française at 10 P.M., thus creating for Strether an enforced period in

which to observe him without being able to speak to him because of
the performance.

> It was truly the life of high pressure that Strether had seemed to
> feel himself lead while he sat there, close to Chad, during the long
> tension of the act. He was in presence of a fact that occupied his
> whole mind, that occupied for the half-hour his senses themselves
> all together; but he couldn't without inconvenience show any-
> thing—which moreover might count really as luck. What he might
> have shown, had he shown at all, was exactly the kind of emo-
> tion—the emotion of bewilderment—that he had proposed to
> himself from the first, whatever should occur, to show least. The
> phenomenon that had suddenly sat down there with him was a
> phenomenon of change so complete that his imagination, which
> had worked so beforehand, felt itself in the connexion, without
> margin or allowance. It had faced every contingency but that Chad
> should not *be* Chad, and this was what it now had to face with a
> mere strained smile and an uncomfortable flush." (I, 136–37)

Strether considers the new Chad nothing less than "a strong case, as
people nowadays called such things, a case of transformation unsurpassed" (I, 137). His recollection of the old, awkward, and unattrac-
tive Chad who sailed for Europe three years earlier is that he was
"rough"; now he is "an absolutely *new* quantity" and "actually
smooth" (I, 150, 152). A part of Chad's display of new "refinement"
lies in his "marked streaks of grey, extraordinary at his age, in his thick
black hair" (I, 140).

It is significant that Waymarsh, who was also acquainted with
the old Chad, sits in the same theater box and seemingly sees nothing
in particular by which to be impressed. Strether thereupon surmises
that the "social sightlessness of his old friend's survey marked for him
afresh, and almost in an humiliating way, the inevitable limits of direct
aid from this source" (I, 140). The great irony, however, is that although Waymarsh misses what Strether sees, he also of necessity is not
vulnerable to the young man's "theatrical" orchestrations, which will,
by the end of the novel, propel him into the new "art of advertisement." Waymarsh's lack of response also anticipates the similar nonre-
action by Sarah Pocock, Mrs. Newsome's daughter and the leader of

the second team of ambassadors sent later to rectify Strether. Not only will Sarah echo Waymarsh regarding Chad, she will express fierce, open hostility to Strether for his allegiance to Chad and Marie de Vionnet. More ironic yet, her arrival will enable Waymarsh to become her messenger to Strether, thereby allowing him finally to experience *his* European "second wind" in marked contrast to Strether's: Waymarsh's rejuvenation will result from the support, in the person of Sarah, of the New England "sacred rage."

In sum, Strether's momentous reaction to Chad's great improvement is really as much an index of his *own* change as it is of Chad's: "But oh it was too remarkable, the truth; for what could be more remarkable than this sharp rupture of an identity? You could deal with a man as himself—you couldn't deal with him as somebody else" (I, 137). As Strether here registers his awe at the new Chadwick Newsome, the beauty of James's narrative system is that the "transformation unsurpassed," the "sharp rupture of an identity" is what is happening to Strether himself. The very language with which he inwardly ascribes such profound changes to Chad simultaneously exhibits the evolving benchmarks of Strether's own consciousness.

Another instance of Strether's dramatic consciousness mediating the novel's events can be seen in his intense, crescendoing responsiveness to Madame de Vionnet once he realizes that it is she and not her young daughter Jeanne who is involved with Chad. When he first visits her quarters in the Fauberg St. Germain, for example, he is dazzled by her "possessions not vulgarly numerous, but hereditary cherished charming," by the "old accumulations" the reverse of "any contemporary method of acquisition." They have "the spell of transmission" and "the air of supreme respectability" (I, 244, 245). These rich associations, the complement of her personal charm and manner, give her an attractiveness for him beyond that of Maria Gostrey—up to now the first woman to have put Mrs. Newsome in a less attractive light. In sharp contrast to Miss Gostrey's "museum of bargains" and "pirate's cave," Marie de Vionnet's possessions are "objects she or her predecessors might even conceivably have parted with under need, but Strether couldn't suspect them of having sold old pieces to get 'better' ones" (I, 244–45). Ultimately, then,

> At the back of his head, behind everything, was the sense that she
> was—there, before him, close to him, in vivid imperative form—
> one of the rare women he had so often heard of, read of, thought
> of, but never met, whose very presence, look, voice, the mere
> contemporaneous fact of whom, from the moment it was at all
> presented, made a relation [out] of mere recognition. (I, 252)

Some measure that Madame de Vionnet has greater appeal for
Strether than does Maria Gostrey is clear if we simply recall his comment "You're the very deuce" to the American lady shortly after encountering her at Chester and perceiving her sophisticated knowledge
of things (I, 67). One could never imagine him responding to Marie de
Vionnet in such language. A person of Keats-like "negative capability,"
Strether feels compassion for her cruel domestic situation: she is a
woman with an estranged brutal aristocratic husband living in a culture in which divorce is not an option. Strether's elevated view of
her—and hence of her relationship with Chad—comes to a head in
Book Seventh when he runs into her by chance at the cathedral of
Notre Dame and afterward takes her to lunch at a nearby Left Bank
quay. It is an experience for him of "letting go, of diving deep," more
so than at any time heretofore. He realizes, for instance, that he has
"travelled far since that evening [earlier] in London, before the theatre, when his dinner with Maria Gostrey ... had struck him as requir-
ing so many explanations." In other words, he thought back then in
London that he was letting go and diving deep, and that those actions
had required "explanations."

> But it was at present as if he had either soared above or sunk be-
> low them—he couldn't tell which; ... How could he wish it to be
> lucid for others, for any one, that he, for the hour, saw reasons
> enough in the mere way the bright clean ordered waterside life
> came in at the open window?—the mere way Madame de Vion-
> net, opposite him over their intensely white table-linen, their
> *omelette aux tomates,* their bottle of straw-coloured Chablis,
> thanked him for everything almost with the smile of a child,
> while her grey eyes moved in and out of their talk, back to the
> quarter of the warm spring air, in which early summer had al-

ready begun to throb, and then back again to his face and their human questions. (II, 13–14)

Despite the moment's wonderful Renoir-like Impressionist quality, James's irony remains intact and unsurpassed. Strether's interrogative language about "explanations," for example, proves that, for all his alleged "letting go," he is still temperamentally the puritan compelled to take stock of the propriety of his situation. Indeed, the successive series of questions that define this passage are a kind of secular equivalent to the solemn ceremonial Rogation Days in the religious calendar! But the greater irony still is a structural one. Strether's accidental encounter of Marie de Vionnet at Notre Dame actually functions as a presage to his later chance encounter of her and Chad out in the country when he comes to realize they are sexually intimate.

That later discovery, or "recognition," episode, which occurs in Book Eleventh, is one of the premier virtuoso scenes in the history of fiction. In point of fact, however, it is not a "scene" in James's narrative terminology but rather, as in the foregoing examples, another case of "picture." It is also quite extensive, covering two successive chapters and hence considerably longer than the earlier meditation in the Luxembourg Gardens. To get away from his difficulties (he thinks), he takes a train "selected almost at random" out from Paris and stops, again by sheer chance, at a station that looks promising for his respite with its beautiful "French ruralism" (II, 245). More specifically, his trek through the countryside charms him because he feels as though he were "inside" a rustic Lambinet painting he wished to buy years earlier in Boston but could not afford. Now, however, he has the great compensation of walking within the picture itself: "The oblong gilt frame disposed its enclosing lines; the poplars and willows, the reeds and river—a river of which he didn't know, and didn't want to know, the name—fell into a composition, full of felicity, within them" (II, 247). Near this river is a charming inn, the Cheval Blanc, and it too becomes part of his Lambinet: "The frame had drawn itself out for him as much as you please; but that was just his luck" (II, 252). Strether stands on the small pavilion of this inn that overhangs the water and idly looks out, finally at peace after his daylong amble. "What he saw was exactly the right thing—a boat advancing round the bend and containing a man who held the paddles and a lady, at the stern, with a pink parasol. It was suddenly as if these figures, or something like them, had been wanted in the picture, had been wanted more or less all day, and had now drifted into sight, with the slow current, on purpose to fill up the measure" (II, 256).

In the remainder of the chapter, Strether, Chad, and Marie make the astounding discovery of one another's presence—"It was too prodigious, a chance in a million" (II, 257). The couple's physical attitude and dress make it apparent to Strether that they are away together staying somewhere nearby as the lovers they are and, unbeknownst to Strether, they have been all along. But even so, the couple go through the charade of pretending that, like Strether himself, they have just come out for the day. The three even sit down to an awkward meal at the Cheval Blanc and then together ride the train back to Paris that evening, although, "as night closed in," the couple—especially Madame de Vionnet—are not appropriately attired. Eventually all three grow more silent as the pretense thins with each train-rail mile.

As in the Luxembourg Gardens earlier, this entire episode is a great "reflexion," or meditation, scene, inasmuch as the reader of *The Ambassadors* only gradually realizes that the entire segment covering two chapters is Strether's remembered recollection while he sits in his room the same evening after the train ride back to Paris. He ponders his naiveté, their collaborative deception, and his own distaste for the situation—especially for the couple's "make-believe" in harmony with his wish all along to dress up "the possibility as a little girl might have dressed her doll" (II, 265, 266).

What makes the entire episode-as-picture function as retrospective revelation is that James brilliantly keeps the point of view within Strether the whole time, even when the narrative might strain against it. For example, when Strether first notices something odd about the idyllic couple in the boat, James conveys the process of discovery from the other direction in the following way:

> The air quite thickened, at their approach, with further intimations; the intimation that they were expert, familiar, frequent—

that this wouldn't at all events be the first time. They knew how to do it, he vaguely felt—and it made them but the more idyllic, though at the very moment of the impression, as happened, their boat seemed to have begun to drift wide, the oarsman letting it go. It had by this time none the less come much nearer—near enough for Strether to dream the lady in the stern had for some reason taken account of his being there to watch them. She had remarked on it sharply, yet her companion hadn't turned around. (II, 256–57)

In other words, Chad and Marie recognize Strether first, but their reaction to the recognition is precisely what *focuses* Strether's consciousness and triggers him in the direction of recognizing who they are. He eventually perceives, along with the recognition, that "they would show nothing if they could feel sure he hadn't made them out" (II, 257). Strether has to decide whether to pretend he has not recognized them, and he chooses to call out, gesticulate with hat and stick, and begin all their mutual series of hearty well-mets. The entire section is one of the great scenes in the late James, with even its tiniest natural details subtly supporting the broader themes and conflicts— such as the image of the "drifting" boat insinuating moral looseness; or else the Cheval Blanc hostess offering Strether "a 'bitter' before his repast," which is in effect symbolic of his shock in the next moments before dinner (II, 254). That shock will modulate into a kind of disillusioning chagrin as the evening progresses and Strether eventually sits in his room pondering the entire day, which began with a random choice of a train.

What these exemplary passages and episodes from *The Ambassadors* bring home to us is that the key to James's narratology is his distinct mode of rendering the flux and field of human consciousness. This technique operates in tandem with a third-person point of view focused on his chosen register or deputy, Lambert Strether. In a passage from "The Art of Fiction" that we may wish to revisit more than once for its centrality to James's art, he condenses as well as anywhere in his criticism the essence of the Jamesian novel: "Experience," he writes, is never limited and it is never complete; it is an immense sensibility, a kind of huge spider web of the finest silken threads suspended in the chamber of consciousness, and catching every airborne particle in its tissue. It is the very atmosphere of the mind; and when the mind is imaginative—much more when it happens to be that of a man of genius—it takes to itself the faintest hints of life, it converts the very pulses of the air into revelations. . . .The power to guess the unseen from the seen, to trace the implications of things . . .this cluster of gifts may almost be said to constitute experience, and they occur in country and in town and in the most differing stages of education. If experience consists of impressions, it may be said that impressions *are* experience, just as (have we not seen it?) they are the very air we breathe.[13]

When James redefined the nature and meaning of experience from external reality to "the atmosphere of the mind," he made possible the modern psychological novel of consciousness, anticipating Conrad, Woolf, Faulkner, and others. And he also set down the critical template for his own later work, especially *The Ambassadors*.

5

The Subject and Theme of *The Ambassadors*

Even though Strether's is the central point of view in James's masterpiece, this does not mean that he is the sole central subject matter of the novel. For James, centrality, as expressed in his extended image of "the house of fiction," is always a point from which to look out upon the broader sociocultural world, not merely the spot on which to constrict the focus.[1] In one sense, the most basic subject of any major James novel is the never-ending law of "successive aspects" governing the interconnection of the human community.[2] In his opening preface to the New York Edition, he explains this perennial subject in the following way: "Really, universally, relations stop nowhere, and the exquisite problem of the artist is eternally but to draw, by a geometry of his own, the circle within which they shall happily *appear* to do so."[3]

Within this global framework, however, *The Ambassadors* explores at least two of James's most enduring themes from his fiction: 1) the international subject, or Americans in relation to Europe, and 2) the problems of "human cannibalism" and epistemological bewilderment, or the ethical misuse of one person by another, and the continual shaping and reshaping of reality through consciousness and reinterpretation.

The Subject and Theme of The Ambassadors

INTERNATIONALISM

As we have already seen more briefly, James practically invented the international novel, in which American characters invariably interact or conflict with the labyrinth of European culture. A great number of his fictions, both very early and very late—from "A Passionate Pilgrim" (1871) and "Madame de Mauve" (1874) to *The Golden Bowl* (1904) and "The Jolly Corner" (1908)—explore this fictive terrain. Although one might argue that *Roderick Hudson* (1875) is his first extended treatment of the topic, *The American* (1877) is probably the best all-around choice for the honor, owing to James's conscious intent in this work to fully address the issue. *Daisy Miller* (1878), "Four Meetings" (1877), *An International Episode* (1878–79), "A Bundle of Letters" (1879), and "The Point of View" (1882)—these are all early signature works of Jamesian internationalism; the character Daisy is most auspiciously identified with his special imaginative topic, that of the plight of the international American girl. That story endures in textbooks and in classrooms to this day. But at least as enduring, if not more so, is his first extended masterpiece in the international novel, *The Portrait of a Lady* (1881), whose heroine, Isabel Archer, is a deepened and transmuted version of the successful figure of Daisy Miller.[4]

James's international fiction can be thought of as the "second frontier" in our literary history: when it was published it seemed to predict and accompany the completion of the westward settlement, and the American psyche thereby began to gravitate back toward its European "memory." In general, however, James's international subject eventually came to transpose imaginatively into the deep and archetypal paradigms of innocence and experience, of nature and art, of the ethical and aesthetic consciousness, of freedom and determinism—in other words, into some of his other most recurring subjects. James's international fiction ultimately recapitulates the deep structure of universal polar or dialectical questions, which clarifies why he returned to internationalism in his major-phase period with *The Wings of the Dove* (1902), *The Golden Bowl* (1904), and *The Ambassadors,* as well as in numerous tales. No single novel anywhere in his large corpus more directly and successfully presents these deep polar explorations than does *The Ambassadors,* as we shall see in a later chapter.[5]

What ties Lambert Strether to both Daisy and Isabel from the earlier period is his quintessential American innocence and, as with Isabel especially, his predisposition to idealize others. Like Isabel, too, Strether is highly imaginative, the keynote for both his attractiveness and vulnerability to deception. Although he does not hail from New York State, as do Daisy and Isabel (and also James himself), he shares with Isabel a highly refined moral consciousness, which in his case is part of his cultural birthright as a New Englander. Indeed, much of what makes his character distinctive yet wholly American is just his combination of New England puritan, imaginative idealist, and cultural innocent. Like James's greatest American female heroines, Strether has no direct knowledge of our national financial life "downtown" within the bowels of corporate America. This bears directly on his innocence as well as on the calculating presence of certain others in the novel who do understand that world: Mrs. Newsome, her son-in-law Jim Pocock, and ultimately Chad himself. In this respect, Strether seemingly resembles James, who admitted more than once an ignorance of American business, as in his memorable letter to the wife of Robert Louis Stevenson. "[M]y ears tingle with pain," he confesses, "so abnormally *not* am I a man of business or acquainted with the rudiments of any business transaction whatever. I have always had a constitutional incapacity for everything of the sort and an insurmountable aversion to it, and circumstances have happened, from the first, to confirm me in my habits of ignorance and helplessness."[6]

Although an examination of James's *Notebooks* and dealings with literary agents and publishers would surely render this declaration disingenuous, there is at least a broader representative truth about it. James was never the amateur and dilettante in these areas that, say, his father, Henry Sr., was, but neither was he like his grandfather, William of Albany, whose business acumen in textiles created the family fortune. Strether, it may be said, is far less knowledgeable and "at home" in business dealings than was Henry James himself; however, like James, he is spiritually an alien to that world. This aspect of Strether helps to explain why he is unwilling to name for Maria Gostrey the

"vulgar domestic" article that the Newsome factory complex in Woollett manufactures (I, 60)—vulgar in the sense of common, perhaps,
rather than distasteful, although Strether's reluctance to speak of it allows for dual meaning. In 1900, when the events in the novel occur
(and also when James was composing it), Strether's enduring innocence, while recognizably national, is also becoming somewhat
anachronistic. That is, in *The Ambassadors* James is treating the later
era of American culture that arrived after the heroic period of the New
England conscience, the era of such abolitionists and transcendentalists
as Emerson, Thoreau, and Theodore Parker, who struggled against issues like Negro slavery. As seen in his sobering remarks 30 years after
the Daisy Miller phenomenon, James came to believe that the innocent
phase of American experience was largely past.[7] Strether's innocence is
at once in the process of becoming outdated and yet therefore all the
more compelling, a combination that gives the entire novel its special
affective "nostalgic" tone, not unlike that in Cervantes's *Don Quixote*
or Mark Twain in, say, *Old Times on the Mississippi.*

The other American characters in the novel, however, are more
symptomatic than Strether of the *actual* stamp or plight of American
culture at the turn of the century. Waymarsh, for instance, is a lawyer
bitterly estranged from his wife who hates the relaxed pace and aesthetic ambience of Europe. In Paris, he frequents the reception room
of the American bank in the rue Scribe where, like Hurstwood in
Dreiser's *Sister Carrie,* for example, he pores over the American news-
papers that James, in *The Bostonians* and elsewhere, found so de-
plorable. Only when Sarah Pocock comes to counteract Strether's sup-
posed retrogradation to Paris and pleasure does Waymarsh feel
buoyed up with a mission of his own and a new compatriot with
whom he feels at home. A measure of his practicality being different
from Strether's can be found in his early insightful remark "You're being used for a thing you ain't fit for. People don't take a fine-tooth
comb to groom a horse." But then Strether's reply turns out to be
equally prescient: " 'You'd like them, my friends at home, Waymarsh,'
he declared; 'you'd really particularly like them. And I know ... I
know they'd like you!' " (I, 109–10). Both men's declarations are superb instances of narrative foreshadowing.

Maria Gostrey and John Little Bilham are far more generous versions of a character type James invariably deprecates in his earlier fiction, the Europeanized American. In *Daisy Miller,* for instance, Frederick Winterbourne's severance from his American roots is what ultimately causes him to misjudge and reject Daisy. And in *The Portrait of a Lady* the deformed characters of Gilbert Osmond and Madame Merle arise from their European veneer and hostile alignment against Isabel's native spontaneity. In 1900, however, James's awareness of the less idealistic phase of American culture inclined him to soften his earlier reprobative view of the Europeanized American. He did this because, first, that figure could no longer serve thematically as the automatic perversion of native goodness, and second, because *The Ambassadors,* unlike James's earlier fiction, primarily embraces Europe. To be sure, both Maria and little Bilham carry some residual traces of the Jamesian Europeanized American type: Maria is shrewd and worldly and, like Gilbert Osmond, a collector; little Bilham is at least passively deceitful, as is apparent when he looks Strether "full in the face" and informs him that Chad's relationship to Marie de Vionnet is "a virtuous attachment"—knowing full well that Strether will assume this means that the two are not sexually intimate (I, 180). Yet both characters are, in the end, warm confidants who deeply affirm Strether and wish him well. Maria's regard for him is certainly all tied up with the attractive elements of his "fine-tooth comb" sensibility. As for little Bilham's lie, Strether later admits "it was but a technical lie— he classed the attachment as virtuous. That was a view for which there was much to be said" (II, 299). In general, little Bilham, the young American artist living abroad, is very close to Strether—he is both a surrogate son and a second self. Strether even wishes to make the young man his heir, meager as such a bequeathal would be.

James handles Mrs. Newsome and her daughter Sarah Pocock with great skill; although Mrs. Newsome never formally appears, Sarah's arrival, conduct, and viewpoint constitute her mother's very embodiment. As chief figure in the second ambassadorial delegation sent out by her mother, Sarah might presumably be open for negotiation, but Strether learns that the reverse is true: "he had taken in that [Sarah] had arrived with no proposal whatever; that her concern was simply to show what she had come to receive. She had come to receive his submission, and Waymarsh was to have made it plain to him that she would expect nothing less" (II, 196–97).

Sarah sees no transformation in Chad whatever. Her opinion of Marie de Vionnet, moreover, is unequivocal: "Do you consider her even an apology for a decent woman?" she asks with sarcasm (II, 202). The entire uncomfortable scene with Sarah and Strether in Book Tenth—which occurs before Strether accidentally espies Chad and Marie in the countryside—enables Strether to take a fresh look at Mrs. Newsome through her daughter's moralistic intransigence. In fact, Sarah herself underscores the point: " 'What is your conduct,' she broke out as if to explain—'what is your conduct but an outrage to women like *us*' "? (II, 199). "Us," of course, means her and her mother. It also means moral American womanhood, extending outward presumably from New England. Sarah is especially outraged by Strether's high compliments regarding Marie de Vionnet's character. "You talk to me about 'distinction'—*you*, you who've had your privilege?—when the most distinguished woman we shall either of us have seen in this world sits there insulted, in her loneliness, by your incredible comparison!" (II, 202–3).

As Sarah continues on, Strether comes to realize that she and her mother are one: "These were the very words of the lady of Woollett—he would have known them in a thousand; her parting charge to her child" (II, 203). All of this—Sarah's presence and ultimatums as well as Mrs. Newsome's abrupt cessation of letters to him—enables Strether by the conclusion of the novel to summon up his answer to Maria Gostrey's inquiry about the status of his relationship with Mrs. Newsome. At the very beginning of the novel it was Maria who first witnessed Strether's high encomium to the Woollett lady. She now asks if Mrs. Newsome is "different" for Strether. He replies that "She's the same. She's more than ever the same. But I do what I didn't before—I *see* her" (II, 323). Readers of *The Ambassadors* feel that they, too, have come to see New England's Mrs. Abel Newsome.

The American men other than Waymarsh, little Bilham, and Strether himself are represented by Jim Pocock and Chad Newsome. Although a relatively minor figure, Jim conveys the post-transcendentalist decline of American culture in his stance as an American businessman abroad who imagines Paris to be a sexual playground. He tells Strether that he does not blame Chad one bit for wanting to stay with a French woman. "Why I want to come right out and live here myself. And I want to live while I *am* here too" (II, 84). Jim's words are a brilliant parody of Strether's own poignant germ speech, "Live all you can." Not surprisingly, Strether finds even Jim's vaguest innuendos "as aggressive as an elbow in his side" (II, 88). Jim entirely dissociates himself from his wife's mission and thinks of his trip as a "regular windfall." Moreover, "he didn't know quite what Sally had come for, but *he* had come for a good time" (II, 83). By the same token, Strether perceives that Jim is out of the loop of what "was essentially a society of women" (II, 83), since he is cut off not only from the world of civilized taste but also, obviously, from the strict censoriousness of the Newsome women. Yet Jim makes it clear he understands the calculating power of his wife and mother-in-law: "They ain't fierce, either of 'em; they let you come quite close. They wear their fur the smooth side out." And warming to his analogy: "They don't lash about and shake the cage ... and it's at feeding-time that they're quietest. But they always get there" (II, 86–87). Both Jim and the two ladies are thus American cultural benchmarks. The fierce moral fervor in Sarah and her mother is no longer attached to a great cause like abolition. And the cliché of Jim's good-time trip is a far cry from the world of Emerson, Thoreau, or even the mildly hedonistic Washington Irving.

Next to Strether, the figure of Chad Newsome is culturally the most interesting—at least on the American side. Chad more than anyone, except perhaps Marie de Vionnet, illustrates the profound ambiguity associated with Paris itself, the "jewel brilliant and hard" that "seemed all surface one moment seemed all depth the next" (I, 89). Strether's awestruck response to Chad's change actually recapitulates this very concept, for as Strether gazes at him he seems to see someone "marked out by women" and an "irreducible young Pagan" (I, 153, 156). But then this "Pagan"—like the jewel of Paris—most iridescently expresses himself like the "gentleman" he looks; he merely asks, with mixed amusement and disgust, if Woollett really thinks "one's kept only by women" and adds, to Strether's discomfiture, "I must say then you show a low mind!" (I, 159).

Throughout *The Ambassadors*, Chad remains an elusive element. Sometimes that elusiveness is literal and physical, as when Strether is several times informed that the young man is out of town, virtually always at a time when Mme. de Vionnet, too, is gone. Only after the Cheval Blanc recognition scene does it come home that their mutual absences have not been coincidental. James, incidentally, shows great skill in not making it obvious to first-time readers that the two are off together, although, like the good writer he is, he also provides the evidence that they are. Chad's elusiveness while with Strether comes across in the way he reacts to Strether's enthusiasm. For instance, when Strether says of Marie that "She's wonderful," Chad instantly replies, "You don't begin to know *how* wonderful!" in an overtone that makes Strether uneasy, as if the young man were exhibiting an "unconscious insolence of proprietorship" (II, 68). A different facet of Chad's elusiveness is shown later in Book Eleventh when he and Strether are conferring on the balcony of Chad's apartment in Boulevard Malesherbes. Strether in effect invites Chad to reject Sarah's pressure and even to put the burden on his own shoulders, comparing himself to a camel who "double[s] up my fore legs ... when he gets down on his knees to make his back convenient" (II, 219). But Chad somehow keeps coming round instead to the issue of what Strether himself, by his change of allegiance, will then have to give up: "Well, at your age, and with what—when all's said and done—Mother might do for you and be for you.... What it literally comes to for you, if you'll pardon my putting it so, is that you give up money. Possibly a good deal of money" (II, 220).

The reader senses here that Chad is testing the waters to evaluate Strether's greed. Strether, however, is by temperament devoid of an iota of acquisitiveness and thus similar in that respect to certain other central characters in Henry James, such as Fleda Vetch in *The Spoils of Poynton,* Merton Densher in *The Wings of the Dove,* and of course Isabel Archer. But the same conversation insinuates that such absence from cupidity is *not* the case with Chad, or else why would he recur to it so? And this helps the reader intuit that perhaps Chad really is a bona fide American Woollett Newsome after all! Strether gradually becomes so frustrated with Chad's perplexity at "what [Strether] *gains*" by his position that he reproaches the young man for having "no imagination. You've other qualities. But no imagination, don't you see? at all." Whereupon Chad turns the tables right back on Strether: "But haven't you yourself rather too much?" (II, 225).

This entire scene is extremely revelatory, for Strether truly is a person all but overendowed with imagination, whereas Chad's lack of it is symptomatic of his place in a different, later, postheroic American culture. The same difference between the two men also suggests that Chad's European transformation, a major driving force in Strether's whole change of viewpoint, has all along been primarily a product of Strether's own imagination. That possibility also suggests why, for instance, neither Sarah nor Jim sees Chad as new and improved, and even why little Bilham had once confessed to Strether that he actually preferred the earlier, awkward Chad.

Finally, Chad's jewel-like elusiveness is most fully expressed at the end, in Book Twelfth, when he informs Strether that he is leaving France and has embraced advertising. Strether attempts the last and most ardent of his appeals to Chad's obligation to Marie: "You'll be a brute, you know—you'll be guilty of the last infamy—if you ever forsake her" (II, 308). Although Chad protests that he has no intention of deserting Mme. de Vionnet, Strether senses glibness and repeats his entreaty: "Let me accordingly appeal to you by all you hold sacred" (II, 311).

Chad once again, from Strether's viewpoint, protests too much and instead steers the discussion toward its close by announcing his newfound enthusiasm for advertising—"the great new force."

> "It really does the thing, you know."
> "Affects, you mean [says Strether disconcertingly] the sale of the object advertised?"
> "Yes—but affects it extraordinarily; really beyond what one had supposed. I mean of course when it's done as one makes out that, in our roaring age, it *can* be done.... It's an art like any other, and infinite like all the arts.... In the hands, naturally, of a

master. The right man must take hold. With the right man to work it *c'est un monde*" (II, 315–16).

"*C'est un monde*"—indeed, poor Strether's "whole world" is made topsy-turvy again. One last time, as the "iridescent object," the "jewel brilliant and hard," Chad Newsome seems "all surface one moment, all depth the next." For his European transformation now appears possibly to have been a quintessential case of masterful American proto-advertising. If that is so, it was accomplished only with Strether's contributing imagination, his tribute to the "virtuous attachment."

As often with James's novels, the number of "pure" European characters of real significance is small compared to Americans and Europeanized Americans. In *Daisy Miller,* for instance, the only significant European is the simple Mr. Giovanelli, who walks about Rome with Daisy against convention. In *The Portrait of a Lady,* with its great number of Europeanized Americans, Lord Wharburton, Isabel's first suitor, is the only significant European (i.e., English) figure. In *The Ambassadors,* we find there are only the somewhat minor figures of Gloriani, the sculptor, and young Jeanne de Vionnet, along with the major personage of Mme. de Vionnet. Gloriani, however, is thematically significant as an opposing cultural presence to Strether. It is in Gloriani's home and garden that Strether utters the great germ speech. James's decision not to make the setting the home of an expatriate American artist like James McNeill Whistler, as it was in reality, tells us he wished to reinforce the contrast between America and Europe in this, the core thematic episode of the novel. Strether first experiences the "sculptor's eyes" probing "the deepest intellectual sounding to which he had ever been exposed" (I, 197). But he also comes quickly to feel a sense of alienation from Gloriani's seductive milieu, as when he objects that "You've all of you here so much visual sense that you've somehow all 'run' to it. There are moments when it strikes one that you haven't any other" (I, 206). "Any moral," little Bilham explains to the others. As always with Strether, however, the puritan in him exists alongside the man of great imagination. When Strether later sees Gloriani again at another party, he realizes that the two essentially have nothing in common. The contrast between New England America and urban France is strongly evident in Strether and Gloriani.

This is not the case, however, with Strether and Mme. de Vionnet; the fierce national and cultural opposition lies rather between Madame de Vionnet and Mrs. Newsome/Sarah. We have seen already how thoroughly she captivates Strether. The first time he meets her, in Book Fifth at Gloriani's home, he is struck by her "common humanity." Although he recognizes and is pleased that she seems not at all an "alien" figure—metaphorically "neither Turk nor Pole" (I, 213–14)— he still finds great difficulty somehow in placing her within the compass of his Woollett sensibility. James is never more in serene command of his hero's "gropings" of consciousness than at this juncture in the novel: Strether opines that the lady "oh incontestably, yes—*differed* less; differed, that is, scarcely at all—well, superficially speaking, from Mrs. Newsome or even from Mrs. Pocock. She was ever so much younger than the one and not so young as the other; but what *was* there in her, if anything, that would have made it impossible he should meet her at Woollett?" (I, 212–13).

What, indeed! The final answer to that question is, like so many asked in James's text, the entire European experience of Lewis Lambert Strether, a process intact from "Strether's first question"—the opening three words of the book (I, 3).[8] Strether's educative process is tethered strongly to his warm response to Marie de Vionnet, a woman he senses immediately must preclude "with the others, any freedom used about her. It was upon him at a touch that she was no subject for that" (I, 210). The irony here is that, in Gloriani's vaguely sexually decadent atmosphere, this woman alone stands out for Strether as singularly respectable. One understands his enthusiastic assent, therefore, to little Bilham's later pronouncement regarding the couple's "virtuous attachment."

At the same time, Marie de Vionnet also comes to affect Strether as possessing a particular elusiveness not unlike Chad's. She too has that quintessential jewel-like iridescence: "She fell in at moments with the theory about her he most cherished, and she seemed at others to blow it into air. She spoke now as if her art were all an innocence, and then again as if her innocence were all an art" (II, 115–16). Since the jewel concept was first predicated of Paris, perhaps it is appropriate that this woman who embodies Parisian culture and history conveys similar associations. The persistent enigma, however, is that whereas Paris in the jewel conceit is identified with Babylon, Marie instead suggests to Strether the utmost respectability—more so than Gloriani, Miss Barrace, and her crowd in general.

The momentous Cheval Blanc discovery basically resolves this contradiction by revealing Marie as at once Chad's sexual partner, yet also a respectable woman from other than that of a New England puritan point of view. After the chance encounter in the countryside, and subsequently at dinner, Marie, who has always spoken a "charming slightly strange English he best knew her by," begins to lapse "wholly into French ... with an unprecedented command of idiomatic turns ... [so] that he could but lamely match." This change in her has the effect of "fairly veiling her identity" for Strether (II, 260–61). That "veil" is quite possibly her nervously induced psychic wish at such an embarrassing moment, although the reader cannot really know this without direct access to Marie's consciousness.

Strether's parting interview with her in Book Twelfth is poignant in that she no longer has quite the same power over him nor, even more obviously, over Chad. And yet Strether's admiration for her is never discarded: "he could trust her to make deception right. As she presented things, the ugliness—goodness knew why—went out of them" (II, 277). Strether can now even acknowledge his prior projections onto just about everything hitherto, when he wryly contemplates "the general spectacle of his art and his innocence, almost an added link and certainly a priceless ground for [the two of] them to meet upon" (II, 278). This art-and-innocence language—quarried from James's "central intelligence" and then filtered through his "deputy"— is of course the same language we saw attributed earlier to Mme. de Vionnet herself!

In the final interview itself, however, Strether apprehends for the first time a stricken, abandoned woman, fearful of her impending loss.

> She was older for him tonight, visibly less exempt from the touch
> of time; but she was as much as ever the finest and subtlest crea-
> ture, the happiest apparition, it had been given him, in all his
> years, to meet; and yet he could see her there as vulgarly trou-
> bled, in very truth, as a maidservant crying for her young man.
> The only thing was that she judged herself as the maidservant
> wouldn't. (II, 286)

Marie recognizes that her "only certainty is that I shall be the
loser in the end" (II, 288). As for Strether, it seems to him "almost ap-
palling that a creature so fine could be, by mysterious forces, a creature so exploited" (II, 284). The reader senses in this exchange that
Marie's "certainty" really means that she shall "lose" both Chad and
Strether at the same time—the two men reflecting perhaps her dual
need not only for the love of eros but also for agape. In either case,
Marie's "common humanity," the first sign by which Strether knows
her in Book Fifth, is powerfully and ironically fulfilled by this conclusion. Inasmuch as both Strether and Mme. de Vionnet are fundamentally predisposed to give to others rather than take from them, they
each differ from the other American, Europeanized American, and European characters in the novel. In that respect, if only momentarily,
they overcome the profound continental divide in James's international map.

Final brief mention should be made of the international contrast
between Mamie Pocock, Jim's younger sister and part of their en-
tourage, and Jeanne de Vionnet. The dichotomy between the European *jeune fille* and American young girl is of course a recurring motif
in earlier James. Here it becomes a minor though deftly executed
theme. Mamie, as befits her Jamesian credentials in the tribe of Daisy
Miller and Bessie Alden, so to speak, is far more emancipated than her
European counterpart, the well-bred convent figure epitomized in
Jeanne. Their situations in the novel contribute acutely to its internationalism. Jeanne, whom Strether early and briefly supposes may be
Chad's love interest, charms him greatly with her sweetness and de-
meanor. However, when her mother later discloses to Strether that she
and Chad have arranged a marriage between Jeanne and a certain

Monsieur de Montbron, Strether is taken aback and disconcerted by the cold insensitivity attending this European practice, even though Jeanne herself submits obediently. Mamie Pocock, by contrast, impresses Strether as mature beyond her years and even as someone not necessarily on the same side as her sister-in-law Sarah and Mrs. Newsome. Strether eventually comes to wish she might marry his young *confrère* little Bilham, the penniless bohemian artist. James leaves that issue totally open-ended, but it is intriguing that the last we hear of little Bilham at the conclusion of the novel is that he has joined Mamie, the Pococks, and Waymarsh on their holiday excursion to Switzerland. The emblematic contrast embedded in the figures of Mamie and Jeanne is a "signature" of sorts that evokes the earlier James; at the same time, it now assumes a subordinate role in the more complex fiction of his major phase. Hence it contributes to James's "true dialectical inquiry" so typical of his best international fiction, early or late.[9]

"HUMAN CANNIBALISM" VERSUS EPISTEMOLOGICAL BEWILDERMENT

Christof Wegelin has pointed out that *The Ambassadors* "explore[s] the possibilities of two radically different systems of morality represented by America and Europe."[10] The book is also, he reminds us, a novel of "initiation and conversion," in fact the "story of the making of an American cosmopolitan,"[11] and hence profoundly autobiographical in tone despite its known origin in William Dean Howells's comments. Wegelin further observes correctly that "The capacity for liberal appreciation is what distinguishes Strether from the rest of the Woollett clan."[12]

What governs these special powers of "appreciation" is, as I have suggested before, a moral imagination analogous to Keats's idea of "negative capability." It is the capacity and willingness to subsume oneself generously into the experience of otherness—whether as other persons or as something like the impinging gestalt of one's environment. For Keats, negative capability is, of course, not a moral but a poetic gift, chameleonlike in its Shakespearean versatility. In James, however, it assumes the character of a moral faculty, although inevitably it is found only in someone with a heightened imagination, such as Strether, Maggie Verver (of *The Golden Bowl*), or Fleda Vetch (of *The Spoils of Poynton*). Strether's moral capacity in this dominion is revealed not so much in his lingering puritanism abroad as in his refusal to exploit others for his own benefit. In more traditional philosophical terms, this morality suggests the famous Kantian categorical imperative of treating others as ends rather than means. Unlike in Kant, however, but again like in Keats, this humane faculty is the elegant refinement not of rational thought but of imaginative power; it is less categorical, so to speak, than it is experiential. The hostile opposite human conduct to this ethics-of-appreciation is what may be called "human cannibalism," or the predisposition to use others exploitatively for one's gains or pleasures. The perennial conflict between these two competing modes of conduct is one that is found throughout the fiction of Henry James.[13]

Strether unwittingly articulates his own ethic, though not arrogantly, in the novel's concluding words, during his final exchange with Maria Gostrey. When she attempts to persuade him not to return to America and offers him her loving "service," he demurs:

> "But all the same I must go." He had got it out at last.
> "To be right."
> "To be right?"
> She had echoed it in vague deprecation, but he felt it already clear for her. "That, you see, is my only logic. Not, out of the whole affair, to have got anything for myself." (II, 326)

Strether here formulates his decision as a "logic" by which he probably means something like the geometry of his volte-face in the period of the four months since he first sailed over. That is, how can he suddenly give up Mrs. Newsome, preside over Chad's exploitation of Marie despite his own strenuous efforts against it (in direct antagonism to Mrs. Newsome), and then allow himself to be the sole person who reaps the benefit?

The Subject and Theme of The Ambassadors

It is obvious, however, in the earlier scene on Chad's balcony and in innumerable other scenes in *The Ambassadors* that Strether's decision really has comparatively little to do with "logic," at least by comparison with, for example, the irreducible core of his own character and temperament. Not only will Strether not use people as means for his gain, he seems incapable of *any* self-aggrandizement. This deep truth about his character is just what makes the famous "Live all you can" germ speech so ironic, but then it is also precisely why *he* uttered it, along with his lamentation about its being "too late" for him to "live."

Strether's ethic of renunciation is also an avenue into understanding his powerful attraction to Mme. de Vionnet. During his last interview with her she tells him, despite the inexorable "certainty" of her doom, "that it's not, that it's never, a happiness, any happiness at all, to *take*. The only safe thing is to give. It's what plays you least false" (II, 282–83). Such language makes her Strether's kindred spirit. There is no doubt throughout the novel that he has attributed Chad's improvement to her selfless agency on the young man's behalf, much as, alternatively, he has attributed his son's death to the fact that he did not give of himself to the little boy.

Strether's eventual judgment of Chad reinforces the same point. After the extraordinary encounter with the couple at Cheval Blanc, he perceives during the embarrassing and enervating charade on the train back that Marie de Vionnet is the sole person who pours herself into keeping up the false front (while speaking nervously in idiomatic French, one assumes). Strether that evening in reflection divines that "Chad in particular could let her know he left it to her. He habitually left things to others, as Strether was so well aware, and it in fact came over our friend in these meditations that there had been as yet no such vivid illustration of [Chad's] knowing how to live" (II, 264). The same assessment of Chad is repeated in Book Twelfth while Strether is en route to see Marie de Vionnet for the last time, having been summoned by her, he believes, with Chad's strategic permission: "Chad was always letting people have their way when he felt it would somehow turn his wheel for him; it somehow always did turn his wheel, Strether felt, oddly enough" (II, 278).

Chad's use of others—of Marie de Vionnet in these highly charged circumstances, of Strether himself in others—is but thinly disguised by its veneer of passivity. Like Gilbert Osmond in *The Portrait of a Lady,* Chad achieves his goals precisely by manipulating others without overt or aggressive ostentation. In this respect, then, his choice of advertising is probably a propitious one. And the fact that Strether associates this use of other people with the young man's "vivid illustration of his knowing how to live" tells us that Strether's *own* conception of "living," so poignantly voiced back in Gloriani's garden, is a totally different mode of conduct from Chad's.

The "human cannibalism" theme is also at least highly inferential beyond these three characters. Mrs. Newsome and Sarah both implicitly and explicitly use others—first Strether and later Waymarsh—as means to their own common end. Little Bilham, on the other hand, is not intrinsically an exploiter, even though he does collaborate in the hoodwinking of Strether. Even then he wishes to clue Strether in, as when he tells him at Gloriani's that "you're not a person to whom it's easy to tell things you don't want to know" (I, 202). The delicate type of situation between little Bilham and Strether is one that is heightened still more in the case of Strether and Maria Gostrey. Her intimacy with Parisian mores coupled with her warm feelings for Strether puts her in a well-nigh impossible situation. Strether already knows that Maria, an old schoolmate of Marie's, does not have the high opinion of her that he does. When Miss Gostrey therefore abruptly leaves for the south of France in Book Sixth shortly after Chad introduces Strether to Marie, I suspect she wishes to avoid the position, as Strether's designated European guide, of having to tell him that Chad and Marie are sexual lovers. Were she not falling for Strether herself, Maria could undeceive him. But as things are, she is in the classic "shoot-the-messenger" position, especially since she intuits the rivalry between herself and the lovely expressive Comtesse de Vionnet (James's "central intelligence" emphasizes this inchoate rivalry by conferring on the two women virtually the same name, Maria [Gostrey] and Marie [de Vionnet]). Miss Gostrey can only let Strether find out for himself. The reader, however, can infer the consanguinity between her situation with Strether and that of little Bilham's from the following parallelism: 1) little Bilham departs abruptly from Gloriani's garden just after Chad comes over to introduce his "friend" Marie; 2) Miss Gostrey departs abruptly from Paris in the early stages of Chad and Marie's calculated solicitations with Strether shortly thereafter.

The generic principle of "liberal appreciation" identified by Wegelin and embodied in Lambert Strether not only carries with it a moral sensibility opposed to human cannibalism. It also presupposes—at least if the character in question is James's "center" of consciousness, or "deputy"—both the glory and liability of experiencing epistemological bewilderment. Such bewilderment cuts both ways because the same agency that gives shape to reality, the heightened activity of consciousness, is also what allows for besetting confusion and eventually outright dupery by others.

Paul Armstrong has addressed this concept brilliantly in his extended chapter "Reality and/or Interpretation in *The Ambassadors*,"[14] a discussion that features Strether's situation as "hermeneuticist"—or systematic interpreter—of a world and reality in constant flux. Because he gives himself over to the "composing powers of consciousness," Strether is thereby a "double" for James's own point-of-view narratology.[15] Moreover, by virtue of his constant "gropings," which James dramatizes, Strether is in a real sense fighting for his moral life. As Armstrong clarifies: "Interpretation is itself a moral activity for James because understanding others can lead to ethical self-awareness (as it does for Strether) and to a justifiable moral choice (although perhaps not a necessary and certain one)."[16] Armstrong further explains:

> In Woollett the world may have seemed stable, determinate, and independent of interpretation—"real," pure and simple—because the "categories" and "terms" that made it up were never radically questioned. Strether's bewilderment in Paris reveals that his earlier reality was only an interpretive construct, a framework of assumptions and hypotheses now cast into bold relief because they have been surprised.[17]

Strether's moral journey is above all a valiant attempt to reconcile suspicion and faith—"to understand," or "to unmask"[18]—a task well-nigh impossible because of others' manifold disguises and because of Strether's American proclivity to faith in the postheroic national period. "James never forgets," writes Armstrong, "that the meaning-making activities of the mind are always situated in a field of cultural codes that are both limiting and enabling. But unlike some of the more radical postmodernists, James never doubts that consciousness is the foundation of the world of signs. This is the classicism in his modernism. It also suggests his humanism."[19]

But the problem with even the most heroic "Stretherian" attempts to balance suspicion and faith is that "their balance is at best tenuous and subject to infinite permutations."[20] Such shiftings of the sand and earth of reality—reminiscent, again, of Mark Twain's changing alluvial banks in *Old Times on the Mississippi*—compel Strether to quest for some validation of Chad's virtuous attachment and, as Armstrong puts it, to "justify his faith in [Marie de Vionnet] as a genius of civilized graciousness."[21] The supreme test comes, of course, after the accidental discovery in the countryside. The shock to Strether is puritanical in the sense that he assumed these two were platonic lovers. But a far deeper shock, I believe, is his realization, instantaneous with discovery, that Chad and Marie have deceived him all along for their own ends. And yet not even this discovery of reality breaks down the pattern of Strether's primary role in the novel as a meaning-endowing hermeneuticist. Armstrong addresses this point insightfully: "Even when Strether confronts reality, James is more interested in how his hero understands than in what he sees. Strether learns the truth about Chad and Madame de Vionnet not by facing unmediated facts but by following out the implication of various clues."[22]

Strether's most impressive moral activity after the Cheval Blanc epiphany is his rededication to the virtuousness of Chad and Marie's attachment—despite the loss of his own prospects with Mrs. Newsome, Chad's emerging lack of interest or commitment, and even Strether's own disturbed "spiritual stomach" at the discovery itself (II, 265). Faced with obligations on every side, Strether must somehow negotiate the conflicts between what Armstrong terms, in the parlance of phenomenology, "his self-for-himself and his self-for-others." And in that framework "one standpoint's good may be another's evil."[23]

For Woollett, Strether is the ambassador who has betrayed his duty; for Marie de Vionnet, he is her last source of help in her attempt to keep Chad; for Chad, he is the latest unwitting ally who can "turn his wheel."

What he is for himself, at the end, can be measured by his final insistence to Maria Gostrey that "to be right" he must not "have got anything" for himself. The same morality of duty-to-another fully animates his final attempt to dissuade Chad from leaving Marie: "You owe her everything—very much more than she can ever owe you. You've in other words duties to her, of the most positive sort; and I can't see what other duties ... can be held to go before them" (II, 313). Commenting on these words, Armstrong proposes that

> The norm Strether invokes here is existential—the care one person owes another for care received. Freedom is James's other highest value. Care and freedom are intrinsic rather than extrinsic values—grounded on the structure of experience, not derived from social convention. They are consequently universals. But they do not resolve once and for all, in an unequivocal manner, every question of judgment and conduct. They are infinitely variable in the ways they can be pursued.[24]

Admittedly, one cannot claim that epistemological bewilderment is the direct *cause* of Strether's "existential" and "intrinsic" norm. One can claim, however, that it is the profound *condition* of his rectitude at the end of *The Ambassadors*. To rephrase all this a bit more technically: the constant reinterpretation of reality by the composing powers of consciousness is something without which one cannot achieve the existential morality of a character like Lambert Strether; just as, for example, for St. Augustine the freedom of the will is something without which a person cannot be saved, even though it does not, in itself, save a person. In any event, Armstrong concludes most appropriately that "James's bridge over the darkness is the ceaseless meaning-making of consciousness.[25]

Such consciousness, moreover, is wedded to Strether's honor. For like much of James's fiction of renunciation (and much of Jane Austen's), *The Ambassadors* is about honor. It is not the sort of honor defended in duels but the kind men and women defer to whenever they *honor* their commitments. Mrs. Newsome, to be sure, would not say that Strether has honored his, but the reader simply cannot agree with her as long as her consciousness is not the novel's center. And even if it were, the same reader would then have to evaluate her morality as "extrinsic" if it were derived primarily from social convention, as it seems to be.

6

Ideas in *The Ambassadors:*
Pragmatic Psychology and Philosophy

Henry James was not a writer of "Ideas" in the sense that his friend Henry Adams was or else as were such various post-Jamesian novelists as D. H. Lawrence, James Joyce, and Saul Bellow. And in terms of the major American novelists immediately preceding him, James was less a *philosophical* writer along Melvillian lines than a *psychological* one along Hawthornian lines. It is, in fact, James, in his 1879 critical biography *Hawthorne,* who identifies Hawthorne's keynote as literary psychologist and moralist. Characterizing at once the "originality" and "genius" of Hawthorne's *Twice-Told Tales,* James declares,

> They are moral, and their interest is moral; they deal with something more than the mere accidents and conventionalities, the surface occurrences of life. The fine thing in Hawthorne is that he cared for the deeper psychology, and that, in his way, he tried to become familiar with it.... The author has all the ease, indeed, of a regular dweller in the moral, psychological realm; he goes to and fro in it, as a man who knows his way. His tread is a light and modest one, but he keeps the key in his pocket.[1]

This assessment of Hawthorne also enunciates James's own literary program in 1879—except for his wish to replace Hawthorne's preoccupation with allegory with his own sociocultural interaction among the characters. Still, the moral and psychological complexity at the level of an individual character's experience remains the same. That very complexity became even greater—more "neo-Hawthornian," if you will—in James's late work, after his need to exhibit doctrinaire realism had grown less urgent.

James's profound kinship with Hawthorne's "deeper psychology" is also the feature T. S. Eliot stresses in his celebrated 1918 essay. "There are other points of resemblance," observes Eliot, "not directly included under this [deeper psychology], but this one is of first importance. It is, in fact, almost enough to ally the two novelists, in comparison with whom almost all others may be accused of either superficiality or aridity."[2] In the same essay, as we saw earlier, Eliot compliments James for possessing "a mind so fine that no idea could violate it."[3] In the sense, therefore, that James was a predominantly psychological rather than philosophical novelist, Eliot's dicta with respect to James are consistent with and even comparable to James's view of Hawthorne. In other words, both James and Hawthorne believed that ideas were subordinate to character and psychology.

Today, however—roughly 120 years since the publication of James's *Hawthorne* and almost 80 years after Eliot's memorial essay on James—the criticism of James's fiction in terms of philosophical doctrines, including those of Kant, Nietzsche, Wittgenstein, Husserl, and many others is widespread.[4] So the issue today is not whether James's fiction is *ultimately* relevant and connected to philosophers who lived after he did or, as with Kant, whom James neither knew nor acknowledged; clearly his fiction is relevant. Rather, the issue is how to evaluate those contemporary ideas that may have found their way into *The Ambassadors* from James's personal interest or consanguinity.

Alan W. Bellringer makes an excellent case for the omnipresence of Matthew Arnold's concepts in *The Ambassadors*, especially such recurrent Arnoldian ideas as the "disinterested free play of the mind," the "dedication to culture," the rejection of "provincialism" in favor of becoming a "cosmopolite," and even James's and Arnold's precisely qualified partiality to French culture.[5] James's knowledge of Arnold's literary and cultural criticism is as easily documented as is his high opinion of it. However, what remains distinctive and typical about James's fiction is that he digested such influential ideas and invariably subordinated them to character or to a subjective state of mind. Even so, James distributed—aslant—a number of overtones and nuances of Arnold's thought throughout *The Ambassadors*. One example is the resonance between Strether's metaphor of the "receding train" in his germ speech and Matthew Arnold's "withdrawing roar" of the sea in "Dover Beach."[6] Alwyn Berland believes that the conflict between Mrs. Newsome and Madame de Vionnet (a dichotomy noted in the last chapter) dramatizes the opposition between the dual—and dueling—concepts of "Hebraism" and "Hellenism" Arnold enunciates in his tract *Culture and Anarchy*.[7] Such direct ideological equivalencies are unlikely in James. Nevertheless, Bellringer's view that Strether's "tolerant and open-ended approach to people is the main secret, surely, of his charm" is most accurate, as is Strether's representation of an "elevated, detached observer as the true penetrator of experience."[8] Both of these features Bellringer attributes indirectly to the thought of Matthew Arnold.

The extent of Arnoldian thought in James is debatable, but there is at least one figure whose entire matrix of ideas was far closer to James both personally and intellectually than Arnold's or anyone else's; in fact, James openly acknowledged the relationship of this figure's ideas to his fiction. This figure is his famous brother William James. The interweave between William's ideas and Henry's fiction is not one of direct formal influence but something much closer, that of quintessential embodiment—like vitamin C and the orange. James's actualization of William's ideas means that, in their case, the conceptual ideas are not so much "digested" (as with Arnold or others) but exist in a prior apposition so complete that Henry's work and William's thought mutually explicate one another. And what this means, in turn, is that when Henry most fully embodies William he is also being distinctively "Jamesian" in just those ways that one may also express in terms other than those of William's thought—or any one else's. No other set of ideas bears this kind of embodiment-relationship to Henry James's late fiction.

We must remember that before his development of philosophical pragmatism after 1900, William James was the greatest later-nineteenth-century psychologist (he lived just prior to Freud) and the author of the first classic textbook in the field, *The Principles of Psychology* (1890). Susan Griffin in "The Selfish Eye, Strether's Principles of Psychology" shows conclusively that Strether's fundamental activity of perception parallels William James's "functionalist" theory of "visual perception—that of a unified stream [that] illustrates the fullness and intricacy of Strether's interactions with his world."[9] William James's analysis of perception in *The Principles* was an important corrective of the earlier "associationist" credo, embraced by John Locke, David Hume, and Alexander Bain, for example, all of whom either viewed the percipient as passive in the presence of sensory stimuli or else proposed that the stream of thought is a series of distinct ideas; one could say that they assumed both positions in the sense that passive perception gives way to a series of ideas "about" the content of perception. We can sense quickly how such views have bearing on Henry James and *The Ambassadors,* inasmuch as Strether as the "point of view" figure has long been recognized as "the prototypical Jamesian perceiver."[10]

But as Griffin points out, Strether is *not* passive in his observations; rather, the "active, interested, attentive nature of [his] functional perception means that in the act of seeing, Strether shapes his world and his past."[11] His "self-interested" activity of perception is "selfish" only in the generic sense that perception is the reverse of being neutral: the percipient *attends* within the sensory flux to just those elements that constitute his *interest* and, in the same process, "moves toward discrimination and analysis"; Henry James, that is to say, does *not* describe "how Strether uses some higher faculty to synthesize crude perceptual building blocks into a complex whole."[12] To put it another way, he does not simulate a sort of "two-stage" procedure of the mind in the tradition of Locke and the earlier empiricists; rather, as Griffin explains it, "his understanding comes *as* he composes his visual picture" in the functionalist mode proposed by William James.

Griffin clarifies further: "[Strether's] selfish eye is not the mark of a villain because it is not an organ peculiar to Strether. He does not rationally decide to see as he does—indeed he is usually not aware of the way his interests direct his perceptions. Instead, Strether's pictures are structured by the very conditions of seeing."[13]

Griffin cites as exemplary episodes Strether's first and subsequent viewings of Maria's and Chad's apartments, especially the various ways in which "[his] stream of perception flows toward discrimination" and the fact that his "problem-solving process takes place *in* the stream of [his] perceptions."[14] Griffin's choices are certainly apt. However, the novel's greatest episode, the encounter at Cheval Blanc, discussed earlier, is likewise a tremendous illustration of Jamesian perception (i.e., that of William and Henry). For example, when Strether on the balustrade of the little country inn looks out on the water, he does not merely "receive" sensory content any more than he thereupon "switches to" analysis and discrimination. It is one continuous perceptual experience borne on the wings, precisely, of his directed self-interest:

> What he saw was exactly the right thing—a boat advancing round the bend and containing a man who held the paddles and a lady, at the stern, with a pink parasol. It was suddenly as if these figures, or something like them, had been wanted in the picture, had been wanted more or less all day, and had now drifted into sight, with the slow current, on purpose to fill up the measure. (II, 256)

These lines begin Book Eleventh, chapter 4. "All day" here refers to the preceding third chapter in which Strether walks inside his "Lambinet landscape" after disembarking the train. In other words, his perceptual flux has been "self-interested" "all day" in the same way it is now as he stands on the water's edge, just prior to "discovering" the couple to be Chad and Marie de Vionnet. A William Jamesian approach to the nature of human discovery in late Henry James is a complex affair, to be sure, but the keynote is that it exhibits neither passivity, on one hand, nor intellection outside the stream of experience, on the other. Indeed, such considerations led me to write the following assessment of this same episode 24 years ago:

Strether actively and radically meets the discovery [at Cheval Blanc]; he enters into a reciprocal relation with it, grafting meaning while receiving in kind; he empties every possible insight about himself, his previous assumptions, the thoughts of the two lovers in having to deal with *him,* and even the imagined responses of those back at Paris, into it.[15]

My commentary here meant to refer not only to the perceptual encounter as such but also to Strether's retrospective ruminations about it after he returns to Paris and, like Isabel in *The Portrait of a Lady,* sits late into the night in meditation. What Susan Griffin's analysis in "Selfish Eye" can drive home, if we but let it, is that even aside from the various planes of reflection and retrospection in James's late fiction, the act of "simple perception" is in fact anything but simple.

Furthermore, the novelist's illustration of William's functionalist psychology is, from a critical perspective, an important point of departure from the sort of relationship to be argued for between his work and Matthew Arnold or, for example, John Ruskin or Walter Pater. The point to remember is that Strether's *fundamental* mode of perception answers to William's *Principles of Psychology.* That is quite a different affair from his echoing this or that specific "idea" found in Arnold, Pater, or Ruskin. It addresses not only what Strether thinks but *how* he thinks: the connection is thereby more pervasive and less dependent on any specific tenet. This relationship also suits with the feature in James noted at the beginning of this chapter: the fact that, as T. S. Eliot understood, he is less predisposed toward inculcating ideas per se than in subordinating them to the rendered ongoing experience of his characters.

Henry James did not actually claim any connection between his own work and *The Principles of Psychology* but owned only to "dipping in [it] just here and there" and to putting off reading William's daunting two-volume tome until there came "a stretch of leisure and an absence of 'crisis' in [my] own egotistical little existence."[16] Thus it is most unlikely that he read any of William's formulations that Griffin cites on functionalist perception that do, nevertheless, correctly "name" Strether's mode of perception throughout *The Ambassadors*. James never set about to incorporate ideas from *The Principles* into his fiction any more than the orange "incorporates" the idea of vitamin C. Nor does this connection end with the intricacies of human perception. The same situation obtains in the broader arena where William James is particularly famous, his formulation of a theory of the stream of consciousness. "As we take, in fact, a general view of this wonderful stream of our consciousness," William declares, "what strikes us first is this different pace of its parts. Like a bird's life, it seems to be made of an alternation of flights and perchings. The rhythm of language expresses this, where every thought is expressed in a sentence, and every sentence closed by a period."[17]

Obviously, Henry James does not embody this formulation simply because he writes sentences, even though the late-Jamesian sentence does seem to resemble William's imagery more than do, for example, Hemingway's short declarative sentences in "The Big Two-Hearted River." Rather, *The Ambassadors* embodies William's formulation here because Henry's narrative system of alternating fluidly from picture to scene (as we saw in chapter 3) evokes precisely William's "flights" and "perchings" within the stream of consciousness.[18] But once again, Henry James did not in all likelihood read this formulation, even though William did point to these sections of *The Principles* as ones Henry might wish to look at.[19]

Scholars of William James all agree that the pragmatic philosophy he propounded in the next decade, from 1900 to 1910, evolved directly from his most important and original ideas in *The Principles of Psychology*. Or perhaps one should say that such scholars agree, not only with one another but with William himself, who constantly made the connection. The 1900–1910 decade is, of course, the same period as Henry's major phase and the one during which *The Ambassadors* takes place. As we just saw earlier, James never stated any connection between his own work and William's *Principles of Psychology*, and yet it is clear that he embodies its most original ideas and formulations. The case is totally otherwise with respect to William's philosophy during the period of the brothers' respective "major phases," both of which occurred from 1900 to 1910: for this time period, Henry James *did* affirm the intimate relationship between his fiction and William's pragmatism.

Henry did not view this relationship between his fiction and William's philosophy as one of prior influence, however. When he read *Pragmatism: A New Name for Some Old Ways of Thinking* (1907) he responded with the kind of "shock of recognition" reminiscent of Melville's sense of his own affinity with Hawthorne:

> I simply sank down, under it, into such depths of submission and assimilation that *any* reaction, very nearly, even that of acknowledgement, would have had almost the taint of dissent or escape. Then I was lost in the wonder of the extent to which all my life I have (like M. Jourdain) unconsciously pragmatised. You are immensely and universally *right,* and I have been absorbing a number more of your followings-up of the matter in the American (Journal of Psychology?) which your devouring devotee Manton Marble ... plied, and always on invitation does ply, me with. I feel the reading of the book, at all events to have been really the event of my summer.[20]

The difference between this response and Henry's to William's *Principles of Psychology* is obviously huge, not only because James's identification and approbation is so unqualified and insistent—though that is striking—but because James is now devouring William's "followings-up" rather than, as before, contritely delaying to read William until he could manage to find "a stretch of leisure."

The most remarkable part of his affirmation of pragmatism is the reference to "M. Jourdain," the titular hero of Molière's play *Le Bourgeois Gentilhomme,* who comes to discover from the "Philosophy Master" that for 40 years he has without knowing it been speaking "prose." Critics who detect only irony in this reference—like those who think Eliot's passage about James's mind being so fine that no idea violates it discredits James—will miss the whole import of the statement. James is saying that William's book identifies his own work, his idiom, his "prose." He is not saying that William's philosophy causes or determines his own work, which would be the case in a situation bespeaking influence. William in *Pragmatism,* like the philosophy master in the Molière play, articulates, or *names,* Henry's prose work. The allusion is stunning when we recall that by 1907 James's prose had long since taken shape from the spoken word due to his practice of first-draft dictation. Moreover, William's own title is *Pragmatism: A New Name for Some Old Ways of Thinking.* To "name" the prose, then, like Molière's philosophy master does, is also to name the "way of thinking." In short, James recognizes the profound connection as one of embodiment, which is exactly the case.[21]

Perhaps we could limit or even discount the importance of this claim had Henry provided this one picture of himself sinking under William's spell and let it go at that. But we find instead that he persists, after the successive publications of William's other two major works, *A Pluralistic Universe* (1909) and *The Meaning of Truth* (1909), in exactly the same sort of identification with the philosopher's thought. And he makes even more explicit its application to his own work. With respect to *A Pluralistic Universe,* he assures William that

> It may sustain and inspire you a little to know that I am *with* you, all along the line—and can conceive of no sense in any philosophy that is not yours! As an artist and a "creator" I can catch on, hold on, to pragmatism and can work in the light of it and apply it.[22]

Again, James's reaction to *The Meaning of Truth: A Sequel to "Pragmatism"* is possibly the most unqualified and comprehensive endorsement of any thinker or cultural sage (such as Matthew Arnold) ever penned by James. And he insists on its connection with his own work:

> I find [*The Meaning of Truth*] of thrilling interest, triumphant and brilliant, and am lost in admiration of your wealth and power. I palpitate as you make out your case (since it seems to me you so utterly do,) as I under no romantic spell ever palpitate now; and into that case I enter intensely, unreservedly, and I think you would allow almost intelligently.... You surely make philosophy more interesting and living than anyone has *ever* made it before, and by a real creative and undemolishable making; whereby all

you write plays into *my* poor "creative" consciousness and artistic vision and pretension with the most extraordinary suggestiveness and force of application and inspiration. Thank the powers—that is thank *yours!*—for a relevant and assimilable and *referable* philosophy, which is related to the rest of one's life otherwise and more conveniently than a fowl is related to a fish. In short, dearest William, the effect of these collected papers of your present volume—which I had read all individually before—seems to me exquisitely and adorably cumulative and, so to speak, consecrating.[23]

These "collected papers" he says he has "read all individually before" were most likely among those "followings-up of the matter" he alludes to in the *Pragmatism* letter. But it is the "cumulative" weight of William's argument that makes him now feel that "Pragmatic invulnerability [has been] constituted."[24] Let us turn back again to *The Ambassadors* with these declarations of apposition in mind.

The rich amalgam of ideas that make up William James's pragmatic philosophy are many and nuanced, and in considering their embodiment in *The Ambassadors* it will be helpful to concentrate on the most central ones.[25] We can begin with the close parallelism between William's rejection of absolutism and preconception in the realms of morality and epistemology and Strether's turning away from the moral absolutism of Woollett. In France, he relocates his moral seriousness contextually instead of a priori, as we saw earlier. Strether himself explains the nature of pragmatic openness to Maria Gostrey late in the novel when discussing Mrs. Newsome's lack of it. He might almost be characterizing William's philosophical opponents:

> That's just her difficulty—that she doesn't admit surprises. It's a fact that, I think, describes and represents her; and it falls in with what I tell you—that she's all, as I've called it, fine cold thought. She had, to her own mind, worked the whole thing out in advance, and worked it out for me as well as for herself. Whenever she has done that, you see, there's no room left; no margin, as it were, for any alteration. She's filled as full, packed as tight, as she'll hold. (II, 239)

Ideas in The Ambassadors

She had worked the whole thing out in advance—this is the keynote of antipragmatic preconception, or "a priori-ism." Strether highlights her "fine cold thought," which evokes William's favorite opponents, the Rationalist school. Her inability to "admit surprises"—an inability so greatly duplicated in her daughter Sarah Pocock that it stands proxy for the absent Woollett lady herself—is again squarely opposed to pragmatism, in which the very nature of any category is that it undergoes constant modification in the light of "consequential" experience. Therefore, when Strether, who is so pointedly unlike Mrs. Newsome or Sarah, feels that Marie de Vionnet "had taken all his categories by surprise" (I, 271), he is revealing a "way of thinking" deeply at one with that of William James and at odds with William's Rationalist opponents. Alternatively, when he utters initially Mrs. Newsome's prescriptive language at the beginning of the novel, telling Maria Gostrey that Chad's unknown companion must be "base, venal—out of the streets" (I, 55), he is momentarily antipragmatic. His language at that moment is as foreign to his natural temperament as is Huck Finn's whenever he speaks the language of acculturated "conscience" while deciding whether or not to turn in Jim.

Eventually, Lambert Strether's "Jourdain-like" mentality, so to speak, results sometimes in passages that amount virtually to William's celebrated pragmatic method. For example, when trying to determine in his mind the quality of Chad's " 'high fine friendship' " with Mme. de Vionnet, he asserts, "[A]s to *how* it has so wonderfully worked—[it] isn't a thing I pretend to understand. I've to take it as I find it" (I, 280, 281).[26] Of course, the irony here, as always, is that Strether must eventually "take it as he finds it" in ways radically unforeseen at present. But his very mentality is what always enables him to readjust, as does James's in his fictive commitment to the drama of the unforeseen to begin with.

Beyond the concepts of the pragmatic method and the opposition to preconception, however, the world of *The Ambassadors* reaffirms William's view of experience itself as an immediate flux that both furnishes material for reflection and, just as important, allows the terms of such reflection to then "feed back" into the ongoing flux. Actually, such feeding back is what William means epistemologically by "consequences," and it is what Henry means by "implications." Such a conception of experience is, of course, most relevant to James's invoked "centre(s) of consciousness," and it also connects closely to those ideas from *The Principles of Psychology* discussed earlier. That is why the following formulation from *The Principles* can serve as the perfect signature for Strether's interior life and drama philosophically considered: "Experience," William James proposes, "is remoulding us every moment, and our mental reaction on every given thing is really a resultant of our experience of the whole world up to that date."[27]

After 1900, William developed philosophical versions of this very idea. One of the most striking is his theory of knowing as "ambulatory relations" set forth in *The Meaning of Truth*. According to William, ambulation is opposed to what he calls "saltatory relations," or "pure acts of the intellect coming upon the sensations from above, and of a higher nature," so that one supposes himself justified in "jumping as it were immediately from one term to another." This is not the case, however, if one's view of human cognition is ambulatory, that is, "made out of intervening parts of experience through which we ambulate in succession." William clarifies his stance:

> Now the most general way of contrasting my view of knowledge with the popular view (which is also the view of most epistemologists) is to call my view ambulatory, and the other view saltatory; and the most general way of characterizing the two views is by saying that my view describes knowing as it exists concretely, while the other view only describes its results abstractly taken.[28]

What William is getting at here is the disparity—so often unacknowledged by philosophers—between a generic knowledge derived from an abstract summarizing of experience, on one hand, and the actual knowing that accrues moment to moment in the process of said experience, on the other. It is a little like the difference between our saying, "Lambert Strether journeys to Europe on behalf of Mrs. Newsome" and the opening chapters of *The Ambassadors*. Further expounding the saltatory/ambulatory dichotomy, William affirms that "My thesis is that the knowing here is *made* by the ambulation through the intervening experiences."[29]

Ideas in The Ambassadors

William James's "concrete" view of ambulatory cognition answers to Strether's "process of vision," as James calls it in his preface, throughout *The Ambassadors*. For William does not just allow for but downright insists on the reality of all the "nuances" experienced in the activity of knowing. For this reason, ambulation is closely aligned with the dramatic nature of perception as examined by Susan Griffin in the novel. And it is also allied with the "ceaseless meaning-making" of consciousness, interpretation, and bewilderment discussed earlier in regard to Paul Armstrong's analysis.

Most of William's very best philosophical ideas can be shown to interrelate with ambulation. For example, his typical view of pragmatism as "cordial" and "unstiffening" relates to the idea that the mind is on friendly terms with each successive part of experience. The same epistemology insinuates a democratic bent to his philosophy as well as to those pragmatists that followed him, like John Dewey. His belief in a metaphysics of pluralism relates to the idea that the mind should resist any seduction by a "saltatory" extrapolation from experience's "intervening parts," each of which deserves to count as real, and the additive aggregation of which is thus necessarily plural. Where *The Ambassadors* constantly realizes this matrix of ideas is in its Jamesian provisionalness of theme and thesis and in its qualification through nuance and unforeseen possibilities of a situation that simply will not remain "fixed." Another of William's consistent metaphysical ideas in the later philosophy is the great importance he gives to phenomena-as-novelty, which is hence unfixed and which is the counterpart to Henry James's corresponding emphasis on the unforeseen in his fiction. As William best explains it, " *'The same returns not, save to bring the different.' Time keeps budding into new moments, every one of which presents a content which in its individuality never was before and will never come again.*"[30]

With so much emphasis on confluence, flux, novelty, pluralism, and ambulation, it is not surprising that William James also challenges the traditional view in Rationalist philosophy regarding the relationship between the apparent and the real in metaphysics. Unlike the Rationalist schools of Descartes, Kant, or his friend Josiah Royce, William believed that the apparent was not "inferior" to the real, since the apparent is, after all, how the real comes to us in experience; besides, the conceptual ideas by which traditional philosophy determines what is real must themselves return to experience to be tested. In *The Ambassadors,* this stress on the apparent is sounded almost like a key signature in music when Strether first feels a vague sense of disconnection from Woollett while standing before the dressing-glass "with a sharper survey of the elements of Appearance than he had for a long time been moved to make" (I, 9). This capitalization of the realm of the apparent, so to speak, does not diminish but ramifies throughout the novel. The relationship between the apparent and the real is expressed in such great touchstone passages as the earlier-discussed jewel conceit—"it twinkled and trembled and melted together, and what seemed all surface one moment seemed all depth the next" (I, 89). A similar relationship is immediately seen in another passage, earlier cited, that describes Mme. de Vionnet's mystery: "She fell in at moments with the theory about her he most cherished, and she seemed at others to blow it into air. She spoke now as if her art were all an innocence, and then again as if her innocence were all an art" (II, 115–16). In both of these instances, there is just no subordination of the merely apparent to the truer reality. Instead, the apparent and the real keep exchanging places and refuse to arrange themselves hierarchically.

Much the same scheme is followed out in the novel in the successive phases in which Strether evaluates Chad. When he first arrives with his memory of Chad from Woollett, he thinks of him mainly as the "wretched boy" (I, 55). But when he meets Chad at the Comedy Française, he is bowled over by the young man, who appears to be "a case of transformation unsurpassed" (I, 137). Strether feels that he "had faced every contingency but that Chad should not *be* Chad.... You could deal with a man as himself—you couldn't deal with him as somebody else" (I, 136–37). Next he compares Chad's new "smoothness" with that of an "irreducible young Pagan," but then the young man modulates from "Pagan" to "gentleman" before Strether's own eyes when he asks if they all think back home at Woollett that "one's kept only by women" (I, 156, 159).

Having thus thoroughly reconstructed his original view of Chad, Strether now gradually reconstructs his own reconstruction. He begins to sense ever so vaguely Chad's exploitation when the young man speaks with a certain patronizing crassness about Marie: "You don't begin to know *how* wonderful!" (II, 68). Then he finds himself stunned when Chad and Marie arrange the marriage of young Jeanne. He sees still more of Chad's predilection toward questions of personal "gain," and he even complains of the young man's lack of "imagination" (II, 225). Then in the wake of the Cheval Blanc discovery he is sharply conscious of Chad's letting others "turn his wheel for him" (II, 278). And by the time the novel draws toward its close, he is pleading with Chad not to desert Marie, while the young man is eulogizing the art of advertising—"*c'est un monde*" (II, 316). Hearing Chad speak this way at this moment, after constructing so many "Chads" in the course of the novel, Strether's "mental reaction," to use William's language, "is really a resultant of [his] experience of the whole world up to that date." The whole world—*c'est un monde*!

The epitome of Strether's re-reconstruction of Chad probably occurs with Marie de Vionnet when he observes her desperation and thinks ruefully about the source of her pain:

> she had but made Chad what he was—so why could she think she had made him infinite? She had made him better, she had made him best, she had made him anything one would; but it came home to our friend with supreme queerness that he was none the less only Chad. . . . The work, however admirable, was nevertheless of the strict human order, and in short it was marvelous that the companion of mere earthly joys . . . should be so transcendently prized. (II, 284–85)

Clearly Chad Newsome has in the course of this novel fulfilled the terms of the Parisian jewel—he is both all surface and all depth. Of course, there is considerable irony in Strether's assessment given his own elevated response to Chad. But Strether is enough of an empiricist to recognize that he has had some role in the "transcendence" of Chad: "Strether had the sense that *he*, a little, had made [Chad] too; his high appreciation had, as it were, consecrated [Mme. de Vionnet's] work" (II, 284). The way Henry James "unstiffens" the traditional relation between the apparent and the real conveys the philosophy of

William James. It is also a distinguishing Henry Jamesian feature in the late work.

William James's doctrine of ambulation connects closely with still another of his philosophical propositions, that of the transitional nature of ideas. That is, conceptual ideas are "transitional" by virtue of arising from immediate experience momentarily in order to reenter it, so that such concepts function as relations—in transit—between different facets of experience. This philosophical proposal eventually led William directly into the doctrine he called radical empiricism, which he prefaces thus in *The Meaning of Truth:* "[My] generalized conclusion is that therefore the parts of experience hold together next to next by relations that are themselves parts of experience."[31]

In *The Ambassadors,* perhaps the most conspicuous example of a "transitional idea" is the expression "virtuous attachment." This is the phrase supplied to Strether by little Bilham in his explanation for why Chad, despite whatever inclinations he may have, cannot abruptly abandon his companion and leave for home. As we have seen already, Strether interprets the phrase to include, if not solely comprise, the idea of platonic love. "Virtuous attachment" then proceeds to undergo constant modification in the light of its consequences in experience. Eventually, for Strether it comes to include, if not solely comprise, the idea of sexual relations. It is a "transitional" idea whose meaning is reshaped in the stream of experience. Of course, that example is not the only one from the novel, but it is a convenient and isolable touchstone. Another transitional idea with a broad multiplicity of facets is the idea of how "to live," which Strether initiates in the germ speech and which in a sense Henry James wraps around the novel as a whole. William James's most famous declaration, found in *Pragmatism,* is probably this one: "Truth *happens* to an idea, It *becomes* true, *is made* true by events. Its verity *is* in fact an event, a process."[32] Perhaps we can say that truth is predicated of all ideas transitionally, and with considerable drama—that is, with "an event." In *The Ambassadors,* truth happens to the idea of how "to live."

The final two examples of the novel's embodiment of William James that I shall suggest will also take us back to the heart of the novel's theme. First, in the great germ speech at Gloriani's home,

Strether declares himself with regard to an imposing philosophical question, that of freedom and determinism. We can gauge the significance of this passage not only by the fact that it appears in the germ speech but by the fact that James added it entirely to his source: the question of freedom arises nowhere in the background incident involving Howells as reported to James by Jonathan Sturges, nor does James bring it up anywhere in his *Notebooks* or in the Scenario sent to Harper's. Only while composing the text did he decide to centralize this passage in Strether's lament.

> The affair—I mean the affair of life—couldn't, no doubt, have been different for me; for it's at the best a tin mould, either fluted and embossed, with ornamental excrescences, or else smooth and dreadfully plain, into which, a helpless jelly, one's consciousness is poured—so that one "takes" the form, as the great cook says, and is more or less compactly held by it: one lives in fine as one can; therefore don't be, like me, without the memory of that illusion. (I, 218)

James chose the germ speech as the repository in which to embed the book's core philosophical question, whether or not we act as free agents. Strether is obviously a character, not the author. Yet even if we do not identify Strether all that closely with James, we can sense that these particular statements about the nature of consciousness and freedom are, for James, unusually authorial. But then again, when Strether goes on to say, "[D]on't be, like me, without the memory of that illusion," we feel we *are* back with the character, with the "mature and distinguished man" who originated, distantly, in William Dean Howells. And in fact, the speech does show up James's distinctive genius in that the character is never subordinate to the ideas: Strether's feeling is that the spectacle and regeneration of life—this episode occurs in April with its mythic, Chaucerian quickening—has already passed him by. His plea to "seize the day" is, characteristically, for some other person and not himself, which also gives the plea its overtone of prefiguration of the novel's ending.

All the same, the passage does have philosophical import apart from Strether's character and circumstances per se. To begin with, the proposition that there are varying degrees and gradations of fixed sensibility and consciousness, from plain to ornamental, in tandem with the concept of freedom as necessary illusion—this is clearly a "mediating" philosophical position between the ancient competing arguments for freedom and determinism. As such, it answers remarkably to the perspective William James takes in his philosophical doctrines, especially "The Dilemma of Determinism" (1898) but implicitly throughout his mature philosophy. What should be stressed is that Strether propounds philosophical "indeterminism"—to use William's term from the essay. The argument is founded, first, in the sheer variety (plurality) of "consciousnesses" Strether invokes together with the conception of freedom as an actual, functioning "illusion." The William Jamesian perspective also guarantees the notion of unforeseen chance, such as in Strether's meeting Marie de Vionnet at Notre Dame cathedral or his encountering the couple in the boat at Cheval Blanc after riding on a train "selected almost at random." This conception of freedom as a functioning illusion in a positive as well as potentially limiting sense is particularly William Jamesian, and it falls in with his justification for belief, despite "the facts" of science, in his famous essay "The Will to Believe" (1898). William, generally speaking, always stresses pragmatism's combination of both tender- and tough-mindedness, and Strether captures just that mediating admixture in his proposition. Even his image of the "tin mould" should put us back in mind with William's insistence that experience "is remoulding us every moment."

What makes Strether's speech to little Bilham about freedom unusual is that it is rare in James to find such a formal and direct engagement of "ideas." That makes it significant, of course, that such ideas exhibit consanguinity with William James. But possibly the best touchstone in the novel for the connection with William is not an ideological passage at all but is one more characteristic of the novel as a whole, since James, as was stressed at the start of this chapter, was more of a Hawthornian than Melvillian artist. The passage I have in mind is the rejoinder Strether makes to the angry accusations about his conduct by Sarah Pocock:

I don't think there's anything I've done in any such calculated way as you describe. Everything has come as a sort of indistinguishable part of everything else. Your coming out belonged closely to my having come before you, and my having come was a result of our general state of mind. Our general state of mind had proceeded, on its side, from our queer ignorance, our queer misconceptions and confusions—from which, since then, an inexorable tide of light seems to have floated us into our perhaps still queerer knowledge. (II, 200–201)

This passage brings us to the very nexus of William James's pluralistic universe, the ambulatory relationship of next-to-next, the confluently related elements of experience, in which—most important—one simply must not distinguish where one cannot empirically divide. The same passage is also pragmatic, of course, in the attitude taken toward a priori preconceptions, but that almost seems minor, for the moment, at least, in comparison to its expression of a William Jamesian coalescing process-reality; the "queer ignorance," for example, is conjoined and coordinated with "perhaps still queerer knowledge" and is expressed through the inevitable water imagery. Strether's statement here in effect recapitulates the rendered and felt world of the entire book. In a similar vein, the fact that *The Ambassadors* begins with "Strether's first question" and ends with "Then there we are" points by itself to the extent to which Henry James adheres to William's world of the ongoing given and "merely" apparent.

7

The Architecture and the
Poetry of *The Ambassadors*

Even though the philosophy and psychology of William James names—like "M. Jourdain"—the distinctive Henry Jamesian elements throughout *The Ambassadors,* it does not quite account for the book as a literary masterpiece, as the rival to Shakespeare, for instance, that writers as different as Graham Greene and Ezra Pound claimed James to be. William James's thought goes far to explain the novel's distinctive character, which is no small affair. However, such thought does not quite comprehend the book as a work in common with the poetry of Emily Dickinson or Edwin Arlington Robinson, the fiction of William Faulkner, Virginia Woolf, or Ernest Hemingway. In this chapter, I wish to discuss the novel as an expression of high art and of the literary imagination.

One place to begin is with a certain statement James makes in his essay "Project of Novel," sent to Harper & Brothers in 1900 for publication in Harper's and the only Scenario of his novels that survives. At the conclusion of this 20,000-word prospectus, which reads at times almost like a novella, he speaks of composing *The Ambassadors* in 12 distinct parts, "each very full, as it were, and charged—like a rounded medallion, in a series of a dozen, hung, with its effect of high relief, on a wall."[1] This heightened sense of the work's underlying structure and symmetry shows that these are qualities James obviously expected *The Ambassadors* to have. Similarly, his comparing it to a series of "medallions on a wall" conveys his hope for the book's high texture, inasmuch as James in his criticism thinks inevitably of painting or sculpture as analogues to literary creation. Although a Jamesian "medallion" could at first put us in mind of a Florentine carving by, for example, Pisano, Brunelleschi, or Ghiberti, I doubt that James himself had them in mind. However, I believe he *was* thinking of a specific painting—Jan Van Eyck's great *Arnolfini Marriage* portrait, with its breathtaking medallion-mirror in high relief on the back wall, a convex malleable mirror conveying intricate strata of self-reflexivity and capped by the artist's signature. But although Van Eyck's *Arnolfini* has been displayed nearby in London's National Gallery since the year before James's birth and was unquestionably seen there by him, there is really no specific evidence that he had this or any painting (or sculpture) in mind for the medallion metaphor.[2] What is indisputable, rather, is his high artistic aspiration for *The Ambassadors* well before his later enthusiasm for its accomplishment after the fact, which he recorded in the New York preface.

Another way of thinking about the art of this novel is to sift through James's words, published the same year as *The Ambassadors,* about another classic novel. *Madame Bovary,* he wrote,

> has a perfection that not only stamps it, but that makes it stand almost alone; it holds itself with such a supreme unapproachable assurance as both excites and defies judgment. The form is in *itself* as interesting, as active, as much of the essence of the subject as the idea, and yet so close is its fit and so inseparable its life that we catch it at no moment on any errand of its own.... The work is a classic because the thing, such as it is, is ideally *done,* and because it shows that in such doing eternal beauty may dwell.[3]

Like *Madame Bovary, The Ambassadors,* too, provides literary history its foundation for the poetic novel of the twentieth century found in Woolf, Lawrence, Conrad, Joyce, Mann, Proust, Fitzgerald, Elizabeth Bowen, and others. Similarly, as I noted early in this study, the late-James novel has strongly influenced modern poetry.[4] We might remark here James's accentuation of Flaubert's technical perfection, and we should not miss his emphasis on the inseparability of *Madame Bovary*'s "form" from its "essence." This formulation of organic unity—a post–Romantic Movement organic unity residing in fiction rather than in poetry—also expresses James's challenge and achievement in *The Ambassadors*.

Quite apart from the archetypal deep structure discussed in chapter 2 and the pairing off of characters examined in chapter 4, the book's underlying structure is complex and elegant. James's "dozen medallions" correspond to its extremely skillful 12-part division, each formally designated a "Book." As successive narrative blocks, James's arrangement is shapely and effective. Book First, a sort of prologue, initiates the theme of Europe. Book Second, split between London and Paris, conveys quickened impressions and clarifies the ambassadorial mission. Book Third first introduces Chad's charming friends, then follows with the delayed, suspenseful "display" of the new Chad. In Book Fourth, Strether opens negotiations with Chad and, feeling inadequate, is reassured by little Bilham that the attachment is virtuous. In Book Fifth, Strether meets Mme. de Vionnet at Gloriani's and afterward delivers the germ speech to little Bilham. Book Sixth finds Strether visiting and aligning himself with Mme. de Vionnet. In Book Seventh, Strether encounters Marie de Vionnet by accident at Notre Dame and, increasingly captivated, has lunch with her, and Mrs. Newsome fires off a telegram recalling him. Book Eighth covers the arrival of the second wave of ambassadors, the Pococks, who seem to see no change in Chad. In Book Ninth, Mme. de Vionnet reveals Jeanne's arranged marriage to Strether, and he experiences a "sensible shock" (II, 129). Book Tenth builds to the hostile interview with Sarah and her ultimatum from Mrs. Newsome. Book Eleventh culminates in the great "recognition scene" in the rural countryside, after Strether has escaped the city and—so he thinks—the impasse of his problems. Finally, Book Twelfth covers Strether's encounters with Marie de Vionnet, Chad, and Maria Gostrey preparatory to his sailing back.

Interestingly, each of these 12 books alternates between two and three chapters until, significantly, the final two divisions: Book Eleventh expands to four chapters so as to lead up to and comprise Strether's recognition and meditation at Cheval Blanc; Book Twelfth extends to a fifth chapter in order to incorporate Strether's final round of visits, so to speak, and his decision to leave for America. Moreover, the sequencing *in* Book Twelfth itself is skillful: the first two chapters carry us through Strether's final poignant exchange with the anguished Marie de Vionnet; the third chapter finds him, as before, talking things over with Maria Gostrey, only now they have mutual knowledge of Chad and Marie's sexual intimacy (Miss Gostrey did not have to become the "shot messenger" after all); the fourth chapter comprises Strether's last vain attempt to persuade Chad to stay with Marie, and the young man's counterdeclaration on behalf of "advertisement"; lastly, the fifth chapter contains Strether's farewell breakfast with Maria Gostrey and his decline of her offer of love expressed as "service," and he refuses to get anything for himself out of the whole business. He does nonetheless admit that he and Mrs. Newsome are through.

The final two books are extremely satisfying for the reader, especially after the "resolute rupture" that concludes Book Tenth in the wake of the fierce enmity from Sarah Pocock. "It probably *was* all at an end" (II, 206)—this is Strether's final thought in Book Tenth, and at one important level this is so, as the novel's ending bears out. But this same prediction is also a skillful example of foreshadowing in reverse, in that Strether is about to experience in the following book his central epiphany in the novel—so things are hardly yet "all at an end" for him! The final division, Book Twelfth, gathers together the novel's major threads and is particularly effective at presenting our last impressions of the three principal characters in Strether's European adventure as well as of Strether himself. To appreciate what James has done, the reader needs to balance the "William Jamesian" nature of the conclusion, the sense that this tale is not—nor can be—over with, on one hand, against the feeling of completion James endows these last two expanded books, on the other hand. The pragmatic world of process is never compromised or undermined one iota, and yet the sense of both a climax and a recapitulation, as in music, is somehow vouchsafed.

If *The Ambassadors* may be compared with a piece of music, its 12-book structure may also evoke some associations with epic poetry. It obviously has not the lofty theme of an epic poem, nor is its hero a great warrior like Aeneas. But Wordsworth had shown that a modern epic could celebrate the growth of a poet's mind, and Milton had used the classical epic chieftain—Satan—as a foil for a newer sort of heroism embedded instead in humanity through Adam and Eve. Strether, in addition to the growth of his mind, most certainly endures his trials and in his own "intrinsic" ethical terms keeps the faith. With such additional examples of the epic form as Whitman's democratic "Song of Myself" and Melville's *Moby-Dick,* the form had already undergone considerable creative modification by James's time, and I do not mean to insist on too extensive a connection between James and the epic tradition. At the same time, the 12 books of *The Ambassadors* do recall at least the formal structure of both *The Aeneid* and *Paradise Lost*—the latter poem, incidentally, figures prominently (though not structurally) in James's earlier masterpiece *The Portrait of a Lady.*

Returning to the subject at hand, James's 12-part structure reveals a brilliant adaptation of the novelist's use of magazine-publication conventions. Always apprehensive about his age's demand for serialized fiction, in this instance James transformed a potential handicap into a triumph. By laying out the novel in 12 books, he was able to allow each to serve for a month's installment in *The North American Review.* F. O. Matthiessen explains the relation of serial form to theme in this regard:

> [James's] subject was well fitted to such treatment, since it consisted in Strether's gradual initiation into a world of new values, and a series of small climaxes could therefore best articulate this hero's successive discoveries. It is interesting to note also the suspense that James creates by the device of the delayed introduction of the chief characters in Strether's drama.[5]

An important measure of James's success in tethering *The Ambassadors* to serialization is the important fact, sometimes overlooked, that once he composed this book he could never again shape his succeeding major-phase novels to the format of serialization; for instance, he lamented to H. G. Wells with respect to *The Wings of the Dove* (1902)—the novel published before but composed after *The Ambassadors*—that "evidently no fiction of mine can or *will* now be serialized."[6] The relation to magazine publication, then, is another facet of the unique "medallions" in *The Ambassadors*.

Daniel M. Fogel makes an excellent case for likening the novel's structure to "a spiral dialectic in which the first and last books are critical for evaluation of the intervening ones and are opposed to the middle books, which present an extreme of opposition both to the original point of view and to the parallel, initiated, wider, wiser, final one."[7] In clarifying this idea, Fogel keenly points out that while Books Fifth through Seventh "show Strether at the antithesis of his original position," Books Eighth through Twelfth "modify the extremity of his position in the middle books."[8] That observation is important, for it indicates that although the discovery at Cheval Blanc is indeed momentous, it is also a subtle trajectory Strether has been traversing unconsciously since the end of Book Seventh, especially in episodes like Jeanne's arranged marriage or Chad's promptings on his balcony to Strether on behalf of personal gain. If looked at momentarily from this broader perspective, we might even say that the train "selected almost at random" (II, 245), which carries Strether to the countryside and thus leads him to the scene at Cheval Blanc, is as greatly the antithesis of chance on a deeper psychic level as it is the epitome of chance on both its literal and conscious levels.

Whether or not Strether's "return, on a higher level, to his point of origin" is specifically "a nearly perfect enactment of the Romantic dialectic of spiral return," as Fogel contends, is less certain.[9] Some part of the discussion might be what one construes his returning "point of origin" to be: America, yes; but does he go back to Woollett? Does that discrimination matter? All the same, when Fogel speaks of the third stage in the spiral dialectic as a "parallel, initiated, wider, wiser, final one," he enunciates the same sense the reader has of a satisfactory completion in the last two chapter-expanded Books, Eleventh and Twelfth. That sense of completion, as I proposed earlier, balances beautifully against the opposing and compelling Jamesian feature of this novel's ongoingness, its stake in process and in William James's philosophical tenet that reality is always "in the making."[10]

The architecture of *The Ambassadors* is not confined to its impressive 12-book structure, however. James's image of "rounded medallions," "very full" and "charged," constitutes a rich metaphor precisely because such works of composition are intricately carved or painted internally but also linked to one another both linearly and synchronistically as "a series in high relief." How does James accomplish this in *The Ambassadors*?

One way is through his use of episodic motif. Like Hawthorne's employment of three great scaffold scenes in *The Scarlet Letter,* James presents a series of balcony scenes in *The Ambassadors* as markers of Strether's process of discovery and bewilderment. The first, at the end of Book Second, occurs when Strether first walks to the Boulevard Malesherbes to meet Chad and sees emerging onto the balcony of Chad's third-floor flat a young man he realizes after a brief moment is not Chad, although like Chad, he suggests youth itself to Strether. This young man turns out to be little Bilham, with whom Strether remains close throughout the novel. Because this balcony scene occurs early, its thickness of meaning is almost surely lost on a reader unless retrospectively revisited. The fact that Strether naturally expects to see Chad and meets instead the charming little Bilham furnishes part of Chad's strategic staging—his impressing Strether with his new Parisian life while "delaying" his own appearance and also Mme. de Vionnet's. But the significance of this scene does not end there. After Strether looks up for a moment at the youth "resting on the rail," the young man "began to look at [Strether] as in acknowledgement of his being himself in observation" (I, 97). This reciprocity of observation can point across the entire length of the novel to the scene at Cheval Blanc, in which Strether himself will rest against a balustrade, gaze out, and discover himself as the object of observation by the couple in the boat who turn out to be Chad and Marie.

Placing little Bilham thus emblematically in Strether's own later role insinuates another theme, the extent of little Bilham's and Strether's spiritual kinship: for little Bilham is both Strether's spiritual son (as Chad never is, though he would be after Strether's marriage to

Mrs. Newsome) and also Strether's own lost youth—the specific subject of his meditation immediately preceding this first balcony episode. Such powerful affinities between little Bilham and Strether in turn aid and collaborate in Strether's deep romantic interpretation of the "transformed" Chad later; symbolically speaking, by seeing little Bilham instead of Chad, he sees little Bilham *as* Chad. James's text conveys this idea beautifully and ironically when, discovering the young man to be someone else, "Strether wondered at first if perhaps he were Chad altered, and then saw that this was asking too much of alteration" (I, 79). Such textual language anticipates Strether's encounter with Chad at the Theatre de Française when he discovers Chad magically "altered." The irony is heightened when the reader realizes that Strether's thought here about "asking too much of alteration" comes from his recollection of Chad's uncomeliness back in America, and at the same time it foreshadows himself agape later at the theater in the face of "every contingency but that Chad should not *be* Chad" (I, 136–37). Finally, Strether's "upward" gaze at Chad's balcony symbolizes what will become his uplifted, elevated view of the young man and his relationship with Marie de Vionnet.

Because this first balcony scene tends to slip by the reader without his or her grasping its depth and complexity, I have chosen to dwell on it somewhat longer than on the other balcony scenes in the novel, which have, nevertheless, a more or less comparable density. In Book Ninth, for example, Strether comes across Mamie Pocock on the balcony off Sarah's salon, where in surprise she "thought you were Mr. Bilham!" (II, 148), whom she awaits. This time, in other words, Strether is the stand-in figure. In the course of their conversation, Strether gains an appreciation of Mamie's "quality" and senses that she alone among the pilgrims from Woollett may side with him regarding Chad's "improvement." Later, at the beginning of Book Eleventh, Strether is now the one standing on Chad's balcony—where little Bilham stood in the first episode—until Chad arrives and joins him there. This later occasion initiates the conversation in which Chad urges upon Strether his gains and losses and Strether in turn laments Chad's lack of imagination. In this scene, Strether is himself "elevated" on the balcony, and his verbal parrying with Chad no longer reflects his exalted projection of the Europeanized Chad so much as it reveals the loftiness of his own sensibility and ethic.

In the great Cheval Blanc countryside scene at the climax of Book Eleventh, Strether awaits his supper by strolling down to the raised pavilion by the idyllic river. He stands against the balustrade, gazes out, "and, though hungry, felt at peace"; therefore "[w]hat he saw was exactly the right thing" (II, 255, 256). After his highly charged indecision before he acknowledges his sighting of Chad and Marie, Strether discerns that "they would have gone on, not seeing and not knowing, missing their dinner and disappointing their hostess, had he himself taken a line to match" (II, 258). Instead, James's narrator tells us, "[O]ur friend went down to the water" and "assisted their getting ashore" just after "they had bumped at the landing place" (II, 258). "Our friend" here is, of course, Strether. This time he must step off the balcony, so to speak, and descend to actuality, the meaning of which is augmented by the "bump" of the boat against the land. Strether is undeceived.

The final balcony scene occurs in the second penultimate chapter of Book Twelfth, when an exhausted Strether comes to Boulevard Malesherbes for the last time to persuade Chad not to desert Marie de Vionnet. As he looks up again at the balcony, "it was as if his last day were oddly copying his first. . . . and a figure had come out and taken up little Bilham's attitude, a figure whose cigarette-spark he could see leaned on the rail and looked down at him" (II, 305). This time the figure is Chad. Strether no longer "sees" little Bilham as Chad; indeed, James's artistry of emblematic motif-and-reversal is complete when Chad, "with promptness and seemingly with joy, called him up" (II, 305). Chad's too casually enthusiastic tone is much the same as the one he showed at Cheval Blanc after the chance meeting; the "promptness" is the sheer opposite of all the earlier suspense and delay tactics. Hence the invitation to "come up" is a lofty ascent Strether no longer feels, wishes for, or believes in.

James's balcony-scene motif in *The Ambassadors* is obviously remarkable inasmuch as it exhibits the way his literary imagination works, but it is also typical of his method and design generally in this novel. For example, Strether's exhaustion at the end of Book Twelfth just noted stands in perfect reversal—and parallelism—to his state when he first arrives. "I was dog-tired when I sailed," he earlier informs Waymarsh, a comment that "had the oddest sound of cheerfulness" (I, 29). That is, he was exhausted when he left Woollett but has felt unaccountably rejuvenated since his arrival in England. At the other end of his adventure, one that has been propelled by his rejuvenation, Strether is again exhausted. Ironically, Waymarsh replies at the beginning in a sort of riposte that "*I* was dog-tired . . .when I arrived" because there "ain't a country I've seen over here that *does* seem my kind" (I, 29). Yet it is Waymarsh, as we have seen, who eventually experiences rejuvenation with the arrival of Sarah and her mission.

Various elements in James's design function in the same way to support his complexity of meaning while endowing his work with formal excellence similar to that which he praises in *Madame Bovary*. The meditation scene in Book Second, for instance, in which Strether contemplates his life's failure, especially when measured against his youthful aspirations just after the war, comes to foreshadow the more extensive and cataclysmic meditation after the Cheval Blanc scene in Book Eleventh, in which Strether must face down his own illusions—"as a little girl might have dressed her doll" (II, 266). This is especially poignant since these illusions seem to serve as some measure of redemption of his earlier missed opportunities. Between those two great meditation scenes lies the germ speech —"Live all you can"—which both reaches backward to the first meditation and extends forward to the second.

James's musiclike leitmotif occurs with certain key issues and terms as well. The reader of the novel finds during the middle books in particular that Madame de Vionnet more and more "thus publicly drew [Strether] into her boat" (II, 94), especially when Sarah and Jim first arrive. A correlative idea is sounded when, for example, Strether is associated with "the sublimer element with which he had an affinity and in which he might be trusted awhile to float."[11] The foundation for this boat-and-float conceit derives, to be sure, from Strether's international journey by steamship across the water and into a different culture, but the eventual function is to lead us into the recognition scene, when Strether's discovery of Chad and Marie in the boat forces him to realize he is *not* ultimately in their "boat" and can no longer "be trusted to float." Instead, he must "bump" against the shoreline of reality.

A less extensive but certainly no less important case of verbal motif occurs when Strether's exhortation "Live all you can" is recalled later by little Bilham with a certain modification: "Didn't you adjure me, in accents I shall never forget, to see, while I've a chance, everything I can?" (I, 278). Little Bilham's rescripting from "live" to "see" has some profound thematic implications, especially when we consider that Strether does not correct little Bilham's memory. Along with the novel's final scenes, this exchange may infer the extent to which the primary act of Strether's life has been to see, which is also why James in the preface, as we saw, emphasizes above all else his own need to render Strether's "process of vision." However, as a purely technical device, the fluctuation from "live" to "see" is also like the modulation in a musical theme, especially when one remembers that eventually Jim Pocock will appear on the scene and exhort to Strether his wish to live it up all he can!

A conceit comparable to the motif of boats and floating is one built around the conceptual matrix of playacting, a motif James also employs extensively in his next novel, *The Wings of the Dove,* but also favored earlier in such works as *The American* and *The Portrait of a Lady*. This idea is introduced early in Book Second when Strether is at the London theater with Maria Gostrey. Strether feels a heightened consciousness of "a world of types" and a "connexion above all in which the figures and faces in the stalls were interchangeable with those on the stage" (I, 53). This idea, of course, presages Chad's "delayed" appearance in the box at the Theatre de Française in Paris, when Strether must take in silently his "transformation" during the performance. The conceit of playacting and its correlative ideas are naturally congenial to Henry James because of his preoccupation with epistemological bewilderment and appearances. At Gloriani's, Strether begins to muse aloud at the sheer beguilement of Paris. Miss Barrace, one of Chad's circle of friends, says in reaction that in Paris "[e]verything, everyone shows." "But for what they really are?" questions Strether. Whereupon Miss Barrace rebuts, "Oh I like your Boston 'reallys!'" (I, 207), a reply that effectively continues the felt world of the "iridescent jewel." A brilliant modulation of this motif takes place after the new ambassadors arrive and Strether finds, to his surprise and chagrin, that Sarah and Waymarsh "were arranged, gathered for a performance, the performance of 'Europe' by his confederate [Mme. de Vionnet] and himself" (II, 105). This performance-reversal comes about precisely because Marie has "drawn him into her boat" in Sarah's sight. Strether's performance, however, is never successful, like Chad's, and Sarah eventually pillories him in Book Tenth. Rather, the ultimate fruition of the performance conceit comes during the final interview with Chad in Book Twelfth when the young man announces himself a student of the new "infinite art" of "advertisement," that is, "[i]n the hands, naturally, of a master" (II, 316). How can poor Strether not wonder whether his "appreciation" of Chad and his new life throughout the tale has been the result of manipulation by the advertising man?

The intricate relationship between motif and theme, between "the form" and "the essence"—to recur once more to James's language for *Madame Bovary*—can be exhibited in a special way if we return once more to the great germ speech, not the preliminary version from the *Notebooks* cited in chapter 1 but this time the entire speech, from the text of the novel. The speech in *The Ambassadors,* far more than even in the 1900 Scenario, has the character of a full soliloquy, except that little Bilham's presence, of course, disqualifies it technically as soliloquy. James, as the poet says, loads his rift with ore, principally by interlacing the rhetorical stages of the speech with figurative language that presumably wells up from within Strether due to the emotion and intensity of the moment.

> It's not too late for *you,* on any side, and you don't strike me as in danger of missing the train; besides which people can be in general pretty well trusted, of course—with the clock of their freedom ticking so loud as it seems to do here—to keep an eye on the fleeting hour. All the same don't forget that you're young—blessedly young; be glad of it on the contrary and live up to it. Live all

you can; it's a mistake not to. It doesn't so much matter what you do in particular, so long as you have your life. If you haven't had that what *have* you had? ... I see it now. I haven't done so enough before—and now I'm too old; too old at any rate for what I see. Oh I *do* see, at least; and more than you'd believe or I can express. It's too late. And it's as if the train had fairly waited at the station for me without my having had the gumption to know it was there. Now I hear its faint receding whistle miles and miles down the line. What one loses one loses; make no mistake about that. The affair—I mean the affair of life—couldn't, no doubt, have been different for me; for it's at the best a tin mould, either fluted or embossed, with ornamental excrescences, or else smooth and dreadfully plain, into which, a helpless jelly, one's consciousness is poured—so that one "takes" the form, as the great cook says, and is more or less compactly held by it: one lives in fine as one can. Still, one has the illusion of freedom; therefore don't be, like me, without the memory of that illusion.... Do what you like so long as you don't make *my* mistake. For it was a mistake. Live. (I, 217–18)

Apart from the pacing of this speech (the narrator says, "with full pauses and straight dashes, Strether had so delivered himself," [I, 218]) and the use of the word "mistake," which sounds like incremental repetition in poetry, James's striking metaphors bind this moment to the novel as a whole, thereby corroborating his contention that the germ stretches successfully from one end of the book to the other. Hence the train that Strether laments having missed, even though it awaited him past departure time, so to speak, is finally "caught" by him later, in Book Eleventh—and is "selected almost at random" (II, 245)—when he rides to the French countryside and eventually chances upon Chad and Mme. de Vionnet conveying an attitude that infers their sexual intimacy. This meeting collapses his lofty interpretation of what little Bilham has called their "virtuous attachment." In other words, the train metaphor points ahead across the canvas of *The Ambassadors* to the great recognition scene, one reminiscent of Isabel Archer's all-night vigil in *The Portrait of a Lady,* and that could, like Isabel's, be similarly described as "obviously the best thing in the book, but it is only a supreme illustration of the general plan."[12]

Next, the imagery of the "great cook" and his "tin mould" for ornamental jellied dishes, although its immediate function is to represent the limitations of freedom, is another metaphor that stretches in both directions by establishing connection with Strether's series of meals that act as benchmarks of his apprenticeship in Europe. First there is his recollection of dining out back home with Mrs. Newsome during the excitement of his very different evening dinner in Book Second in London with Maria Gostrey. Her dress is " 'cut down,' as he believed the term to be, in respect to shoulders and bosom, in a manner quite other than Mrs. Newsome's" (I, 50). Then there is the soft sensual meal on the Left Bank with Madame de Vionnet in Book Seventh after he discovers her by accident at Notre Dame cathedral, a meal that marks still greater initiation away from the puritan ambience of his evenings out with Mrs. Newsome and that also marks, to Strether's surprise, a considerable distance even from his London outing with Maria Gostrey. Still later, in Book Eleventh, there is the meal set for him by the hostess at the Cheval Blanc in the rustic village Strether wanders into. He is "hungry," has worked up an "appetite," and is told by the hostess that "she had in fact just laid the cloth for two persons who, unlike Monsieur, had arrived by the river—in a boat of their own." We recall that the same hostess offers Strether "a 'bitter' before his repast" (II, 254). This next stage of initiation, then, is the awkward meal he shares with Chad and Marie de Vionnet after he accidentally espies them ("too prodigious, a chance in a million," [II, 257]), together in the boat, after which the three must sit down to eat. His "bitter" becomes his "repast," so to speak, and they prolong the pretense, though ever more thinly, by riding back to the city on the train. No wonder Strether later that evening in meditation thinks of Chad and Marie's "make-believe" as "disagree[ing] with his spiritual stomach" (II, 265).

The tin mould metaphor functions as the principal signifier of consciousness and freedom, as we have seen earlier, or, more properly, as both the limitations and felt experiences of human freedom. In the last chapter, I addressed the connection between this portion of the germ speech and the thought of William James and shall not repeat it here. What that discussion and this one point to, however, is James's

astonishing unity-through-multeity—Coleridge's concept of the imagination—found in this speech and in the novel more broadly. James
manages to select the all-too-human moment and weave his philosophical, thematic, and character studies into it through a veritable
poetics of metaphor and motif, a process that suggests, once again, the
linked "medallions" he aspired to in his Harper's Scenario.

Even the metaphor of the clock, whose loud ticking Strether associates with freedom, is implicitly a complex image consistent with
these ideas: for although the clock is rhetorically associated with the
expansive European life, as opposed to New England constriction, the
same image is psychologically associated with the speaker's feeling
that for him it is "too late," which is precisely why the clock ticks so
loudly. The sense that Strether cannot ultimately change his temperament—which is also the sense in which "the illusion of freedom"
sounds its negative note—is captured at the very end of the novel in
Book Twelfth, when Strether humorously compares himself to one of
the figures on the clock in Berne, Switzerland: they came out on one
side, "jigged along their little course in the public eye, and went in on
the other side" (II, 322). Like the actual train rides compared to the
metaphorical trains, the Berne clock diminishes the expectations of
free autonomy proposed by the ticking metaphorical clock. For despite his sense of new personal freedom after he disembarks from
America, despite his fermenting declaration to live, despite his culti-
vating an appetite for Europe, Strether cannot transcend his own temperament, even though fortunately his is one greatly embossed and
not at all "dreadfully plain." No wonder Ralph Waldo Emerson in his
great bittersweet essay "Experience" denominates "temperament" as
one of the "lords of life." At its best, James's execution in *The Ambassadors,* with its systems of metaphor and motif, seems composed like a
web that, when touched in one place, vibrates the entire design.

The novel's artistry and design discussed in this chapter point to
James's legacy in the tradition of Coleridge, one of whose formulations on the imagination was cited earlier. Although Coleridgean aesthetics and theory are associated with poetry and not with fiction,
their special connection with James is profound, in part because James

belonged to the intellectual sea change in the later nineteenth century that no longer tied the literary imagination exclusively to formal verse. This reorientation derives primarily from Coleridge's first principle that the creative imagination as a faculty of mind and consciousness acts independently of metrics or poetic diction and is grounded ultimately in the universal law of polarity.[13] Although Coleridge himself was never particularly interested in fiction, later in the century such writers as James, Turgenev, Flaubert, and Walter Pater conceived prose narrative as condensed, multivalent, and unified as poetry. Rene Wellek's essay on James's criticism is now almost 40 years old, yet his concluding insight cannot be gainsaid. "James alone in his time and place in the English-speaking world," Wellek writes, "holds fast to the insights of organistic aesthetics and thus constitutes a bridge from the early nineteenth century to modern criticism."[14]

There are a great many passages in James's literary criticism that affirm or insinuate the principle of neo-Coleridgean organic unity. Two of the most satisfying that are also among the most direct are these from "The Art of Fiction":

> A novel is a living thing, all one and continuous, like any other organism, and in proportion as it lives will it be found, I think, that in each of the parts there is something of each of the other parts....
>
> This sense of the story being the idea, the starting-point, of the novel, is the only one that I see in which it can be spoken of as something different from its organic whole; and since in proportion as the work is successful the idea permeates and penetrates it, informs and animates it, so that every word and every punctuation-point contribute directly to the expression, in that proportion do we lose our sense of the story being a blade which may be drawn more or less out of its sheath. The story and the novel, the idea and the form, are the needle and the thread, and I never heard of a guild of tailors who recommended the use of the thread without the needle, or the needle without the thread.[15]

We can comprehend immediately from such passages why James would construct the metaphorical system of motifs we have seen in this chapter, or why, in particular, he valued his accomplishment of

Book Fifth's germ speech and felt so strongly that it radiated throughout the novel.

Speaking more generally, the most important point about Coleridge, I believe, is that Henry James recapitulates Coleridge's theory and practice of organic unity, but he does so *minus Coleridge's cosmology,* without, that is to say, any reference by author or work to those spiritual and universal origins of art that Coleridge propounded. If we can just keep this axiom in mind, then R. P. Blackmur's brilliant assessment of James, quoted in chapter 1 of this study, takes on additional meaning and clarification: that his work occupies a moment of "interregnum" between the "Christian-classical idea" and "the rise to rule of the succeeding ideal, whatever history comes to call it."[16]

To the reader who needs to understand the Coleridgean presence in *The Ambassadors* apart from the historical context in which the novel was composed, the best way to proceed is to explore its neo-Coleridgean polarity. Daniel M. Fogel reminds us that "the novel is rich" in "oxymoronic phrases" and replete with such features as the "wonderful paradox in the handling of Mrs. Newsome, whose absence intensifies her identity."[17] If I may be permitted a digression: among the most interesting things about Henry James is his having become today a major touchstone for postmodern theory. He is easily shown to exhibit such conceptual ideas as Jacques Derrida's *différance* precisely because he uses patented features like the "absent-presence," as in the case of Mrs. Newsome. The fact is that his work extends forward into contemporary theory, on the one hand, yet stretches back to reconnect with early-nineteenth-century aesthetics, on the other. This double extension suggests that one could undertake a thesis to link up Coleridgean polarity and Derridian *différance* using James as the "bridge"—to borrow Rene Wellek's term—between them. Were that argument pursued, however, it would be crucial, once again, to underscore my points that James's Coleridgean unity is shorn of Coleridge's spiritual cosmology and that James does *not* exhibit a mind-set that corresponds to contemporary deconstruction or cultural materialism. In any case, this study has not pursued the path of that critical discussion.

James's unity in *The Ambassadors* can be best grasped by our appreciative response to its rich network of polarity, yet also by my clarifying one last time the important distinction between such polarity and the book's William Jamesian principles of flux and pragmatics. A *full* pragmatic reading, for example, might theoretically be endless in its circularity and "roundness," revolving without closure, like the world of process it explicates; or, again, like the old clock at Berne to which Strether likens himself at the conclusion. Such a reading pays the highest possible tribute to the felt life of the novel through the fluid medium of Strether's consciousness, one subject to minute and subtle gradations of perception, nuance, and inference. In William Jamesian terms this is knowing through ambulation.

Polarity, on the other hand, seeks to unify through opposition. It differs, however, from dichotomy or any binary dualism by virtue of involving interpenetration rather than mere juxtaposition. Most important, it is always a life-endowing relation through opposition and, according to Coleridge, the irreducible principle of life itself. The key point for comprehending polarity properly is to grasp the polar relationship in its positive—or, again, life-endowing—nature. One way to do that is with the following thought: genuine polarity always holds that, whenever one pole, or its opposite, is *predominating* at a particular time and place (for perfect equilibrium is not the constant state of things), the dominant pole is fully dependent on its opposite subordinate pole to *be* predominating; in fact, the energy from the nondominant pole is concentrated at *its* opposite! Yet in human understanding, that is precisely the point at which most of us are least inclined to fully appreciate that polarity exists in the first place, and we are inclined instead toward one "side" or the other—toward thinking more along the lines of dichotomy.

In *The Ambassadors,* genuine polarity occurs in the first place in the relationship between what Strether brings with him across the ocean and what he discovers during his adventure in Europe. That is why, for instance, his aesthetic drive, his feelings of guilt and responsibility about his lost son, his sense of lost youth, and his imaginativeness are all matters that define themselves only by response to everything about Paris, Chad, and Marie de Vionnet that is new, unexpected, or different. Unlike Coleridge, James tends not to express himself *ideologically* in polar language, but there are occasions when he comes close to doing so. One instance is an early hint to the reader regarding Strether's character and the complications that await him; "He was burdened, poor Strether—it had better be confessed at the outset—with the oddity of a double consciousness. There was detachment in his zeal and curiosity in his indifference" (I, 5).

Like a key signature for a piece of music, this comes closer than usual to naming the relationship that governs the novel's larger unity, just as earlier the jewel metaphor comes closer than usual to naming the novel's pragmatic rendered felt life. And yet the jewel image itself, if referred back to its *ultimate* principle, may derive from its polarity between "all surface" and "all depth." Likewise, if we understand Strether's astonished appraisal of Chad in the theater box as a "sharp rupture of an identity" to be the copestone for his concatenating responses ever since arriving to "the elements of Appearance"—that relates through polarity.

A vast polar network expands exponentially to the larger issues and themes raised by the book. The relationship between innocence and experience is rendered as polar, as well as its cognate, that between the moral and aesthetic. The international subject of America and Europe, which is correlative to both, relates through polarity: as contraries they exist simultaneously by virtue of each other as well as at each other's expense. Because of this living relation they can transform into each other, back and forth, which they do within the unifying medium of Strether's consciousness. At the same time, the representatives of James's polarity at its international level—Mrs. Newsome on the one hand, Mme. de Vionnet on the other—do not relate in polarity. That is to say, as characters with viewpoints in and of themselves they really *do* clash in dichotomy (or are "polarities" in the common meaning of the word!). But as representatives within James's encompassing international vision in *The Ambassadors*, these two ladies participate deeply in its international polarity. The reason I stress this is that it is obvious to any reader that Mme. de Vionnet emerges as more sympathetic to Strether and the majority of readers than do Mrs. Newsome or Sarah. And what this bespeaks in the larger polarity in which they function is that *The Ambassadors* in its international theme is a case in James of the European pole "predominating" over its new-world opposite, more so than in either of the other two novels of the major phase, *The Wings of the Dove* and *The Golden Bowl*. But when we have such a case of polar predominance, that is just when we must keep hold of polarity itself. The international theme in *The Ambassadors* comprises the initiation and positive response to Europe. But this predominance of the European pole requires its new-world opposite to sustain it. That is why the New England quality of Strether's response to Europe is indispensable to the book's drama, irony, comedy, and melancholia. And it is also why Strether's decision to return home at the end is both appropriate and inevitable.

Another major polarity in *The Ambassadors* is that of freedom and determinism. Strether's celebrated "illusion of freedom" speech has been discussed already in a variety of ways, especially in the last chapter, with William James's doctrine. The equation between the brothers is quickly recalled in the echo between Strether's encompassing image of the "tin mould" and William's "remoulding experience" passage. But again, if we move outward to the universal level of James's unity, the mediation between freedom and determinism, too, has its source in polarity. At his arrival, Strether feels a new "consciousness of personal freedom as he hadn't known for years" (I, 4). This fresh experience, however, depends for its existence and authenticity on his character as irrevocably "set" in a certain way. Moreover, "the illusion of freedom" is a condition both positive and negative in mode and is related ultimately through polarity. The illusion of freedom remains positive in Strether's capacity to entertain alternatives, respond to new impressions, and choose new allegiances, all of which he does. It is negative in that the quality of such alternative-taking, such responsiveness, and such choice affirms anew what is already predetermined and characteristic in Strether's temperament.

There are also, to be sure, some "outside" determinations, ranging from Chad's strategy of appearance and Mrs. Newsome's second team of ambassadors to the chance meetings of Strether with Marie de Vionnet at Notre Dame and of Chad and Marie at Cheval Blanc. All of these external events evince a reciprocal relationship with Strether's character and ultimately participate in James's network of polarity.

For example, the Pococks' arrival redirects Strether's energies to speak in favor of his own conversion, whereas the news he receives regarding Jeanne's prearranged marriage has disturbing intimations for him of insensitivity at odds with his view of the couple. Sarah's antagonism serves to check such disquieting intimations, yet this very apprehension intensifies Strether's fear that the Pococks see only "the same old Chad they've been glowering at across the sea" (II, 111).

Strether makes the trips to both Notre Dame and Cheval Blanc, the sites of the two chance meetings, with the happy expectation of a temporary respite from "the obsession of his problem" (II, 3), and in both cases he is instead taken to the heart of it. The network of polarity in *The Ambassadors* that involves innocence and experience, moral and aesthetic imperatives, America and Europe, and freedom and determinism also correlates to the polarity of nature and art. Like a great piece of music, the Cheval Blanc scene recapitulates this entire network by presenting itself as an extraordinary case of the nature-art polarity. James's commentators all admire his handling of Strether's extended walk through the French rural countryside "inside" the Lambinet painting he could not afford years earlier in Boston, and of the artistic landscape of the quiet river into which the boat of Chad and Mme. de Vionnet floats. James's Coleridgean polarity is most striking in this episode in that everything about it that is articulated and rendered as "art" serves to conspire in Strether's discovery of Chad and Marie's sexual relationship, which is an embodiment of the fundamental requirement and expression of nature. Strether's warm aesthetic response to the scenery-as-art reaches its apotheosis at the sight of the boat—"What he saw was exactly the right thing"—which thereupon throws into light his puritan morality. This major stage of initiation from prior innocence to experience parallels his rediscovery of his present innocence, an innocence that is the terminus of the whole experience-acquiring process that has led him to this appointed time and place. Such is the intertwining nature of polarity.

Book Eleventh's extraordinary instance of James's unity through polarity is nevertheless "only a supreme illustration of the general plan"—to cite one last time James on Isabel Archer's meditation episode in *The Portrait of a Lady*.[18] What is most important, as always, is that we try not to lose hold of what polarity actually is and means, especially in regard to its difference from dichotomy and to its various dualisms that do not correspond to life-endowing interpenetration. In James's best work, such as *The Ambassadors,* the relationships between experience and imagination and between "living" and "seeing," are cases of polarity in which the latter pole predominates. Unquestionably in *The Ambassadors* it does predominate, which is perhaps only appropriate in a book whose international theme favors Europe and whose formal excellence is striking even for James. And yet all great imaginative literature—including, for example, Whitman's, in which the typical polar concentration is the reverse of James's—is a universal expression of energy in polarity with meaning in which meaning predominates. Viewed from this global perspective, Henry James is a case of literature's own concentration predominating below on the exponential scale and network. That is probably one major reason why James is frequently referred to as "the Master" and as the "novelist's novelist." At James's later post-Coleridgean moment in literary history, such designations bespeak the novelist as the equivalent of a poet and *The Ambassadors* as an epitome of both the literary history and the poetry. Even so, the law of poetry as a faculty of mind and not of formal verse remains the law of imagination, which in turn "recapitulates," as Coleridge would say, the law of life—that is, polarity.

8

Some Special Topics

COMEDY OR TRAGEDY?

She sighed it at last all comically, all tragically, away. "I can't indeed resist you."

"Then there we are!" said Strether. (II, 327)

These are the final words of *The Ambassadors,* and as usual with James, they raise certain intriguing questions. These include questions about Strether's indeterminate future plans back home without Mrs. Newsome and his position as editor of *The Woollett Review.* Another is his real reason for declining Maria Gostrey's offer of love—if in fact it is a "reason" as opposed to the unspoken feelings in his 55-year-old heart. Other questions arise, even one of Jamesian craft-as-interpretation: how does Strether's signature expression, "Then there we are!" relate to an earlier one that concludes chapter 2 of Book Ninth, "But there—as usual—we are!"—a phrase likewise spoken to Maria (II, 142)? Further, how does the same expression relate to one farther back, at the end of Book Third, chapter 1: "So there they were" (I, 118)? Does James mean by this iterative phrasing to stress the "horizontal" of Strether's many inquiries and explorations beginning with the opening line, "Strether's first question"? That is, does he mean to infer the absence of conclusiveness in the open-ended, pragmatic world of this novel? On the other hand, does "There we are!" not actually try to sound out a conclusive note? The relationship between the phrase's terminal sense, on one hand, and its contextual meaning associated with open-endedness, on the other, may be an opposition resolved artistically only through polarity. Such reconciliation in turn supports the reader's sense of the narrative as both ongoing and in process while also evoking that feeling of completion—a subject discussed earlier.

A similar type of issue arises with the other language found in the passage, the reference to "all comically" and "all tragically"—expressed by the narrator as a kind of integrated semantic unit with one "sigh," not two different elements or moods. This integration suggests one genre, not two. But even before we think about the novel's possible "blend" of the comic and tragic, attention should be paid, I think, to the important similarity between this passage and the great touchstone passage of Paris as the rotating "jewel" that shows "all surface one moment . . . all depth the next." The connection, I am suggesting, is very close indeed. For just as the jewel's connotation of the apparent-as-real conveys the mysterious felt life of this novel through Strether's consciousness, "all comically, all tragically" evokes the mysterious feel of the Jamesian "central intelligence" in his narration of a comedy that emits tragic overtones. By the same token, just as the surface/depth concept may interconnect *ultimately* through polarity, so too, one might suppose, do the novel's comic and tragic facets.

It is important to point out that from the very beginning of the genesis and composition of *The Ambassadors* James possessed an intuitive understanding of the novel's potential tragicomic mode. In his first notebook entry, dated 31 October 1891, he ruminated about wanting his protagonist to be " 'intellectual,' I want him *fine,* clever, literary almost: it deepens the irony, the tragedy."[1] As he thinks about the Howells figure in the Parisian garden overwhelmed by his sense of everything in life being "too late," he imagines the primary ambience of his "W. D. H." figure in the *Notebooks* to be that of sorrow, of tragedy and irony. Later in the stages of his composition he added more consciously the element of comedy to the novel. To this day, however, all readers of *The Ambassadors* must deal with its beautifully mixed tonal mode. Like *Don Quixote,* which elicits "hard" and "soft" readings, each of which may go in and out of fashion, *The Ambassadors* can modulate from a Freudian "Mourning and Melancholia" text to a sharp comedy of manners tethered to miscalculation, misdirection, and misinterpretation—somewhat like the style of Molière (the creator of M. Jourdain).

Five years later, in the singular Harper's Scenario James entitled simply "Project of Novel," a document discussed intermittently throughout this study, James continues to speak of Strether as "rueful" and to explain the proposed work in this wise: "the whole comedy, or tragedy, the drama, whatever we call it."[2] As we have seen, James preserves this mixed tonal mode right to the very last lines of the novel, when Maria sighs at last, "all comically, all tragically." Her "sigh," we can now say, started all the way back with that of the "W. D. H." man in the garden and was intoned in the earliest version of James's germ—all of which permits us to think by association of Poussin's pensive canvas *Et in Arcadia Ego.* In point of fact, this same parallel with Poussin achieves fruition just where it should, in the great recognition scene, in which Strether's pastoral walkabout in "a land of fancy," culminates in the chance encounter—"a marked drop into innocent friendly Bohemia" (II, 245, 262). Sexuality and deception enter into the pastoral idyll like Death in Arcadia.

Daniel M. Fogel in his conclusion to the masterwork study of James's early tale *Daisy Miller* makes several distinctions about the genre of that work that may have some bearing here. Explaining why he chose "A Dark Comedy of Manners" for his subtitle rather than "A Tragicomedy of Error," Fogel explains,

> The word *tragedy* would suggest that in the end the protagonist— whether Daisy or Winterbourne—achieves some ennobling awareness of the meaning of what has happened and of his or her own shortcomings, and I do not believe that either of the central figures in *Daisy Miller* comes to such a recognition. A tragicomedy, by de-

finition, is a work (usually a play) with a mainly tragic character but with a happy ending, whereas *Daisy Miller* is a work with a mainly comic character but with an unhappy ending.[3]

In *The Ambassadors,* Strether obviously does not die, as does Daisy Miller, but neither is he as comic a character as is Daisy for one very important reason: he possesses vast powers of reflection and consciousness, suggesting an "ennobling awareness of the meaning of what has happened and of his or her shortcomings." These are frequently given a sorrowful or rueful cast in James's "picture" episodes, or in a resonating lament like the germ speech. By the same token, he *is* a comic figure throughout much of the tale, especially in his extended "scenic" conversations with Maria, little Bilham, Chad, Waymarsh, Marie, and Miss Barrace. So although *The Ambassadors* is hardly a tragicomedy in the manner of *Waiting for Godot,* it comes considerably closer than does *Daisy Miller*. It is a twentieth-century work, albeit an early one, in a way that *Daisy Miller* simply is not. It also has self-reflexiveness and rhetorical lyricism that transcend *Daisy Miller,* although *Daisy* has far more than meets the eye. Such self-reflexive lyricism gives the novel a modernity comparable to the romantic irony found throughout the work of Thomas Mann, for example, who wrote very shortly after the late James.

Another novel that can figure into this analysis is James's early masterpiece *The Portrait of A Lady*. In that work, the Daisy Miller type of American girl, personified in Isabel Archer, is given more of a Strether-like consciousness. Hence *The Portrait* ends up with a distinctive tragic overtone, even though the protagonist does not die. *The Ambassadors* is somewhat "lighter" than *The Portrait of a Lady* in this respect, but it is still a work suffused frequently and strategically with melancholia. My earlier reference to Freud's analysis of mourning and melancholia brings up a suggestive parallel. Freud maintained that mourning was the reaction to the loss of a loved person, or else to some abstraction that had taken the place of such a one. For Strether in meditation in the Luxembourg Gardens, this is the loss of his wife and son and by extension "the higher culture" and "the temple of taste" to which he had intended to devote himself (I, 85, 87).

Freud also believed that in mourning there was nothing unconscious about the loss, and this too defines Strether's articulate meditations. In melancholia, on the other hand, the person knows whom or
what he has lost, perhaps, but not what it is he has lost in them; and this
can become an unconscious loss of a love object. Strether's mourning
seems to touch the level of melancholia in the germ speech, especially
when he tells little Bilham, "What one loses one loses; make no mistake
about that" (I, 217–18). There is also some reason to suspect that at the
conclusion Strether is reacting to his loss of Mme. de Vionnet, but his
conscious rectitude in the face of his mission and her intimacy with Chad
cannot permit him to acknowledge the depth of his feelings for her.

Because James is a consummate artist, the special quality of his
tragic sense of life—to borrow Miguel de Unamuno's relevant concept—shines as frequently in casual narrative elements as it does in
highly charged interior meditations. For example, when wandering
pleasantly throughout the rural countryside in Book Eleventh,
Strether comes across an inn, the Cheval Blanc, or White Horse. The
surrounding beauty is part and parcel of his reverie; it even constitutes
a "text." "The text," says the narrator, "was simply, when condensed,
that in *these* places such things were, and that if it was in them one
elected to move about one had to make one's account with what one
lighted upon" (II, 254). The anticipatory irony, here softly under-
stated, is that Strether is poised on the verge of arranging dinner with
the hostess and then stepping up to the pavilion to gaze out languidly
on the river. In other words, he is but a moment away from having to
"make his account" with what he "lights upon" in a way he cannot begin to imagine. But the same passage continues:

> Meanwhile at all events it was enough that they did affect one—
> so far as the village aspect was concerned—as whiteness,
> crookedness and blueness set in coppery green; there being posi-
> tively, for that matter, an outer wall of the White Horse that was
> painted the most improbable shade. (II, 254)

This is James at his best. First of all, the specific confluence of
colors evokes the landscape painting of Emile Lambinet, the painter
whose too-high cost prevented Strether long ago in Tremont Street

from purchasing the canvas. All day today, however, he has had Lambinet for "free," the "frame ... drawn itself out for him, as much as you please" (II, 252). And yet, what does this passage presage but the discovery, literally on the horizon, of once again the too-high cost for him of a Lambinet?

Most important of all, perhaps, is Strether's discriminating and attentive perception—to recall Susan Griffin's approach to James examined in chapter 6—which takes note of the "most improbable shade" painted on the "outer wall" of the White Horse Inn. This detail, in a sense, is where the passage has really been heading and is all the more effective for being introduced as a seeming afterthought; it is prefaced with "for that matter" (which recalls the afterthought rhetoric of the "dead-letter office" in Melville's *Bartleby* or the "extra fare" in Hawthorne's "Major Molineux"). This "most improbable shade" is emblematic of the dark or tragic side of life in an indeterministic world of the unexpected. The Cheval Blanc episode and meditation as a whole comes to represent one of the last major interpositions of the world of shade in this novel.

The high comedy of *The Ambassadors* is usually concentrated in the infinite variety of exchanges between Strether and one or another character. Waymarsh's bolting away from Strether and Maria Gostrey at Chester in his "sacred rage" is an early instance (I, 46). Strether's discombobulation at the sight of Chad's transformation is another, especially when he manifests his discomposure by blurting out before any civilities, "I've come, you know, to make you break with everything, neither more nor less, and take you straight home; so you'll be so good as immediately and favourably to consider it" (I, 147). This is hardly the discourse of the smooth ambassador. When in Book Seventh he espies Marie de Vionnet by chance at Notre Dame cathedral and assumes (or reassumes) that her relation with Chad must be "unassailably innocent" since, "if it wasn't innocent why did she haunt the churches?" (II, 10), Strether commits what Daniel M. Fogel calls a "hilarious Protestant misreading of appearances."[4] Catholics, after all, just may haunt the churches when they feel sinful.

The most sustained comedy in the novel occurs between Books Eighth and Tenth when Strether finds himself drawn into Marie's boat and forced to undertake "the performance of Europe" in front of the antagonistic visage of Sarah Pocock (II, 105). And then, when Strether does manage to get away with Jim, he has to endure Jim's American-playboy-in-Paris theme under the presumption that Strether himself has already embraced the hot life abroad! Even the Cheval Blanc episode manages to blend initial high comedy with its eventual darkening, "shaded" milieu, especially when the boat first begins to "drift wide" and Strether, his decision made, waves his straw hat wildly and is waved at in return. The final encounter, with Chad in Book Twelfth, cannot avoid, so to speak, its comedic edge when Strether has to stand under the post where he once blurted out his intent to take Chad back to Woollett and now must listen, agape, to Chad's hymn to advertisement.

In a newly (and posthumously) published study of *The Ambassadors,* the late Dorothea Krook makes a brief but acute argument with regard to the novel's comic and tragic elements. She proposes that the book is predominantly a comedy but that periodically "tragic or near-tragic" elements try to break in. Krook proposes generally that in literary "border" cases, like this one, comedy becomes tragic by the author's "pressing the issue" so as "to send it over the border into tragedy." Throughout *The Ambassadors,* however, James characteristically chooses *not* to press the issue and thereby deliberately avoids tragedy. Strether accomplishes much of this by patently "defusing" potential tragic elements, sometimes with strategic laughter. Particularly enlightening is Krook's proposal that the farewell meeting with Maria Gostrey "is a perfect instance of potential tragedy being dissolved into comedy," by virtue of Strether's deliberate refusal to "press the issue." This feature becomes clear when we examine the tone and the language of that final exchange between them. Krook does hold, however, that *The Ambassadors* contains some fully tragic segments, the early Luxembourg Garden meditation and the last Cleopatra-like scene with Marie de Vionnet most notably.[5]

Dorothea Krook's argument is very convincing on the score of the last scene at breakfast with Maria Gostrey. Even the iterative phrase "Then there we are!" contributes to the dissolving of what is potentially tragic back into comedy. If I have sometimes stressed the noncomic side of the coin in my discussion, I have probably been influenced by the tone of the germ speech as the central aria radiating throughout the novel in its unity and music. Besides, there is considerable justification from James for this emphasis. It comes not only from his self-talk in the *Notebooks* but from his description, voiced later in the New York preface, of Strether's outburst as "melancholy eloquence."[6]

"NEGATIVE" AND "POSITIVE" AMERICAN REALISM

This topic sounds like polarity, and perhaps it would be if we were to push our investigations so far as to try to account for the ultimate root sources of things. More immediately, however, I am concerned with locating James from a certain angle within the matrix of nineteenth-century American Realism, even though *The Ambassadors* was published just "over the line" into the twentieth century in 1903. When the novelist writes in "The Art of Fiction" in 1884 that "The only reason for the existence of a novel is that it does attempt to represent life" and that "the novel is history," he positions himself in the mainstream of American Realism along with Howells, Twain, and such regional writers as Sarah Orne Jewett, Mary E. Wilkins Freeman, Hamlin Garland, and others.[7] Although James never deviated from his allegiance with the Realist Movement or from what Vernon Louis Parrington called "the beginnings of Critical Realism," critical theory today is largely hostile to the idea of James as merely a realist. Indeed, if it were just a question of "merely," then such hostility would be lessened, since most traditional Jamesians agree that in the course of his career, he evolved beyond the Realist doctrines with which he began. The problem now is that contemporary theory is by and large inimical to literary realism itself. Its epistemology is deemed naive for being wedded to "knowability" and "referentiality," both of which assume wrongly that author and reader share some knowledge of truth and reality. At least as bad is said to be realism's sociocultural alignment with "masculinism" and "humanism," two somewhat unfashionable persuasions.[8]

Many of today's James scholars are greatly influenced by the French theory of Jacques Derrida, Louis Althusser, Helene Cixous, Julia Kristeva, and others; and it perhaps is too much to expect such disciples to take a less biased view of realism in general and the American Realist Movement in particular. What I wish to propose is an idea I have used for many years while teaching James in the classroom. Perhaps it can mitigate in part the disparity between the contemporary views of James's narratology that make him a darling of the academy, on the one hand, and the historical claims of literary history as well as James's own notions about his work, on the other.

My idea is that we distinguish within the Realist Movement and in James himself between "negative" and "positive" modes of realism. Before clarifying this idea, however, let me rehearse very swiftly the goal and milieu of American Literary Realism. Its purpose was fundamentally that fiction portray the actual world for its own sake while avoiding, so to speak, the Scylla of transcendence (the domain of Romanticism) and the Charybdis of scientific law (the domain of Naturalism). Realism put its premium on the close notation of ordinary life, the rendition of a specific geographical region, the dramatization and criticism of social taboos, and the close delineation of individual character—a domain in which James obviously excels. Although the movement overlaps with Naturalism, it flourished in the last three decades of the last century and was influenced by continental rather than English masters—especially Balzac, Flaubert, Turgenev, Maupassant, and, in the case of Howells, at least, Tolstoy. Also for the later James (and later still for James Joyce) Henrik Ibsen must be added for his combination of poetic drama, social consciousness, technical innovation, and the exploration of individual psychology.

"Negative" realism may be said to be present when the principal purpose of the work in question is to show the destructive consequences of a romantic viewpoint. This type of realism is frequently found in Howells and in Twain in such stories as "Editha" and "The Private History of a Campaign that Failed," and in, for example, the Penelope and Irene subplot of Howells's *The Rise of Silas Lapham* and the Tom Sawyer portions of *Adventures of Huckleberry Finn*. In "Positive" realism, by contrast, the writer attempts to render and poeticize the innumerable shades, nuances, and implications of ordinary everyday reality, an effort that culminates, perhaps, in the permutations of human consciousness itself, James's great domain.

In Henry James one generally finds a predominance of negative realism in his early fiction—in such works as "The Madonna of the Future" (1873), *Madame de Mauves* (1874), "Four Meetings" (1877)—than in such later works as *The Ambassadors,* in which positive realism comes to predominate. Interestingly, *The Portrait of a Lady* (1881), rightly felt by most to be the early James novel that best anticipates the late fiction, nevertheless is greatly about the destructive (mainly self-destructive) consequences of Isabel Archer's romantic view of the world. And what that suggests is that negative and positive realism are most frequently woven together and not simplistically divided between one work and another—similar, for example, to Poe's grotesque, arabesque, and ratiocinative elements. All the same, the fact that we cannot simplistically divide the two does not mean we ought not ever distinguish between them nor recognize that there can be different degrees of predominance: *The Portrait,* for example, like *The Princess Casamassima,* published five years later, is fairly well balanced between its negative and positive modes of realism.

The Ambassadors features in Strether a romantic imaginative protagonist akin to Isabel Archer or Fleda Vetch, the 1897 heroine of *The Spoils of Poynton.* All three are disabused of their illusions in the course of time; all three choose at the end some form of renunciation. *The Ambassadors,* we could argue, exhibits a "residual" substructure of negative realism precisely in this central theme of the inadequacy of the romantic imagination to provide an adequate grip on reality, which results in a somewhat distorted assessment of others. However, by the time James came to write this novel, he had as a realist long since discovered the most important feature about any romantic protagonist: namely, that a romantic viewpoint is comparatively uninteresting for being "wrong" and far more interesting for being *real.* That difference, one we can see even in the changing focus between *Daisy Miller* and *The Portrait of a Lady,* for example, is elementary to James's "realistic" art by 1903. The same reorientation—from the romantic view as wrong to the romantic view as real—intensifies James's positive realism. Thus, when in the New York Edition he retrospectively criticizes his early novel *The American* (1877) for its "fatal" deficiency as "arch romance," James goes on to propose his idiosyncratic definition of the real: "The real represents to my perception the things we cannot possibly *not* know, sooner or later, in one way or another; it being but one of the accidents of our hampered state, and one of the incidents of their quantity and number, that particular instances have not yet come our way."[9]

This 1908 statement is indeed idiosyncratic, but it also shows how thoroughly James had gravitated to positive realism by the late phase of his career. That is, he instinctively dramatizes the concept of the real by making it in effect a process of gradual discovery after the manner of such a character as Isabel Archer or Lambert Strether. The "things we cannot possibly *not* know sooner or later" lie in wait because, if we are romantics, we will try, as does Strether with Chad and Marie, to conceal from ourselves the truth of things. James makes this point doubly plain when he goes on to explain that "the romantic" stands for those things "we never *can* directly know; the things that can reach us only through the beautiful circuit and subterfuge of our thought and our desire."[10] Whether or not we concur with James that these explanations expose a fatal flaw in *The American,* they do happen to describe the epistemologies of Isabel and Strether, the protagonists of the two novels James felt were his best.

Positive realism in *The Ambassadors* finds its fullest expression not only in the psychological grasp and complexity of Strether's individual character and temperament but also in the ways James strives to poeticize actuality. We've seen James do this in many of the examples examined in the course of this study, such as the multiple balcony episodes and freighted details like the "improbable shade" on the "outer wall" of the White Horse Inn just discussed. Other examples are the permutations of Strether's consciousness in the strophelike "picture" movements throughout the novel and the "regional" sense of place we get when Strether walks around the medieval wall at Chester, or sits in the Luxembourg Gardens, or encounters Mme. de Vionnet inside Notre Dame cathedral, or walks up Boulevard Malesherbes from the Place de la Concorde toward Chad's flat.

We can also observe a wonderful example of this "poetry of the actual" in James's play with the semantic possibilities of homonyms. For example, in the flush of his new allegiance to Marie and Chad, Strether in Book Sixth declares to little Bilham that "She has simply given [Chad] an immense moral lift, and what that can explain is prodigious" (I, 284). By attributing to Chad's "moral lift" the capacity for "prodigious explanations," Strether gives away the secret to, and unwittingly reveals the complications of, James's narrative invention: that ethics are never separable from the constant fluctuating process of knowing. Therefore, when James in Book Twelfth sends Strether to Chad's flat for the last time on Mme. de Vionnet's behalf and is forced to climb four flights "without a lift," the mimetic explanation is that "the lift, at that hour, [had] ceased to work" (II, 305–6). However, the deeper meaning is surely that Strether no longer can count on the Chad of the "moral lift." Even the physical world of this novel, it would seem, starts to reshape and represent itself in answer to the interpretive world of "prodigious explanations." The same principle is again at work when Strether perceives from below the "more solid shape" of Chad on the balcony in sharp contrast to the substitute shape of little Bilham early in the novel (II, 305). We have already examined this scene in the last chapter; I wish only to add the point that Chad's "solidity" now corresponds to Strether's less luminous interpretation of him.

Such elements epitomize James's literary art of positive realism. By the same token, these same last hours in *The Ambassadors* do not fail to delineate Strether's pain and exhaustion consequent to being disabused of his romantic "subterfuge and desire." In other words, James conveys that certain residual "trace" of negative realism as well. I believe that contemporary James theorists might recover some acceptance and appreciation of James as an American Realist if they would only allow for the elasticity of his realism and of the movement with which he identified his work.

A POSSIBLE "RE-VISION" OF *THE AMERICAN* (1877)

In the first chapter I discussed briefly the composition of *The Ambassadors* as it relates genetically to the germ in William Dean Howells's lament in the Parisian garden of James McNeill Whistler. A study of James's *Notebooks*, his letters, his Harper's Scenario, and even his later New York preface tends to reinforce what the textual evidence already reveals, that he did not feel the need for much revision in the New York Edition. First of all, his conception of the novel was never problematic in the way it was, for example, in the composition that followed, *The Wings of the Dove*, a work more extensively revised.[11] But is there, perhaps, a broader sense in which *The Ambassadors* itself was a revision?

Let me begin this inquiry with his final preface to the New York Edition, the one introducing his last completed novel, *The Golden Bowl*. Because that was his last preface, James formally addresses the broader issue of revision in his collected writings. He explains that, for him, revision usually turned out to be a case not of his painfully having to "re-write" but of a less painful experience of "re-vision," that is, of "seeing [the work] again" on the heels of his own "re-reading."[12]

In the same preface, however, he briefly laments the one great exception to his revision experience, his lingering dissatisfaction with *The American* ("if only one *could* re-write"). The alleged difficulty with *The American,* as we just saw, is his disappointment at its "arch-romanticism"—a topic he had already addressed extensively in his earlier preface to *The American.* Yet now he proceeds to express his gratitude for what he calls "the altogether better literary manners [than *The American*]" of both *The Ambassadors* and *The Golden Bowl*.[13] This final brief allusion to *The American*—made in his preface to *The Golden Bowl*—may tell us something important: that in a certain sense *The Ambassadors* was for him a more satisfying reseeing of *The American,* even though James may not have intended that purpose when he began *The Ambassadors* with the Howellsian germ.

In fact, *The Ambassadors* does seem from a certain angle to be a reconception of *The American*. To borrow the language of Mark Twain, James's 35-year-old business tycoon "squatter," Christopher Newman the westerner, turns into the 55-year-old "dandy," Lambert Strether the New Englander. Both undergo their initiations into Parisian and Gallic culture, each with an opposing mixture of disappointment and admiration—Newman feels more disappointment than admiration, Strether more admiration than disappointment. Each has his male and female confidants: Count Valentin and Mrs. Tristram for Newman, little Bilham and Maria Gostrey for Strether. Perhaps most important, James in the later book was able to distance his personal allegiance from Strether in a way he never quite could with Newman. Hence, whereas in the 1877 novel James thought he "committed romance" by identifying too closely with Newman and his cause, in 1903 he instead *portrayed* a romantic perspective, Strether's. He stepped just the right number of paces away from his narrative "deputy" and treated him with equal measures of criticism and sympathy, much as he did successfully with Isabel Archer in *The Portrait of a Lady*.

To put some of this another way, James was himself patriotically "Howells-like" in his internationalism in *The American,* but in *The Ambassadors* his protagonist originated in Howells himself, and this may have helped free James from being himself too Howells-like: that is, he could be less nationalistic, more cosmopolitan. Besides, James in the 1870s was probably less critically distant from the moral "new man," Christopher Newman, exactly because he *was* a westerner; whereas James was already used to establishing aesthetic distance from his New England characters—as evidenced in his satiric treatment of Rev. Babcock, Newman's traveling companion, in the earlier novel.

To return to the issue of Howells, James conveys *The American* typically in large chunks of conversational speech, like a Howells novel (one of the very few criticisms James later made of Howells was of this narrative method, by the way), whereas in *The Ambassadors* he uses the compositional layering of Jamesian "picture" and digested "scene" to perfection, as discussed throughout this study. Finally, there are for comparison certain highly suggestive elements and details: Newman, for instance, speaks readily of "wash tubs" and "leather" as his business ventures, whereas Strether, in a feature much noted by James critics, never does name for Maria Gostrey the "common domestic article" manufactured at the Newsome Woollett factory (I, 60). Indeed, merely the names "Newman" and "Newsome" could portend the possibility of some sort of connection between these two books. At the beginning of *The American* in a memorable scene, Newman declares his intention to possess, in a wife, "the best article on the market."[14] This opposes Strether's memorable decline of Maria's offer of love by insisting "[n]ot, out of the whole affair, to have got anything for myself" (II, 326).

There is also extremely resonant language in the two later prefaces to these novels that invite the reader's comparison. James's preface to *The Ambassadors* is replete with the language of "ease," of how, that is, the novel seemed to write itself for him—"Nothing is more easy than to state the subject of *The Ambassadors*," he begins, before turning immediately to the germ. And after remarking again and again on the absence of difficulty in composing this book, he concludes, "Fortunately thus I am able to estimate this as, frankly, quite the best 'all round' of all my productions; any failure of that justification would have made such an extreme of complacency publicly fatuous."[15] Compare that comment with the following evaluation from the preface to *The American:*

> I seem to recall no other like connexion in which the case was met, to my measure, by so fond a complacency, in which my subject can have appeared so apt to take care of itself. I see now that I might all the while have taken better care of it.[16]

For this reader, at least, the language and sentiment from these two prefaces infer a deep affinity between the two compositional situations, one resulting in unhappiness, the other good beyond hope. Those differences bore fruit in two novels with very different cultural critiques. In *The American,* James juxtaposes a morally corrupted "French" Europe against the innocent and untutored but morally "straight" American. In *The Ambassadors,* he sends his innocent American to Paris and Europe in order to discern the expansive possibilities of European culture and the corresponding moral narrowness and hubris of his American society back home.

In sum, James's lasting pleasure with *The Ambassadors* never wavered from his first Howellsian germ, and his choice of it as the best of his novels suffuses his preface in counterpoint to *The American,* the problem-laden novel with which James had a self-confessed identification and emotional tug. Ultimately, these two books evoke the gifted youth and serene maturity of James the writer and the various stages of "re-vision" between them.[17]

AMBIGUITY IN *THE AMBASSADORS*

The subject of ambiguity in the fiction of Henry James has by now become somewhat time honored, if not anachronistic, similar to Hawthorne criticism. One measure of its persistence in James scholarship is the fact that there are two studies of his work with the identical title *The Ambiguity of Henry James*. One of them is a 1971 book-length analysis by Charles T. Samuels, the other an extended criticism first published in 1934 and years later much revised by Edmund Wilson.[18] Although *The Turn of the Screw* is surely the text permanently associated with the problem of ambiguity in Henry James—are the ghosts real or does the governess's neurotic psyche project them?—there are periodic phases in James criticism during which one or another work from his canon is submitted to the question of ambiguity. Is Isabel's return to Rome at the end of *The Portrait of a Lady* affirmative or depressing? Is there really vampirism in *The Sacred Fount* or is the narrator crazy? Is Basil Ransom a hero or just the worst possible sexist villain in *The Bostonians*? Does *The Figure in the Carpet* have anything like an objective correlative? Is James "rhetorically" consistent in *The Aspern Papers* and elsewhere?[19]

Fortunately for readers of James, Dorothea Krook's last published article, *"The Ambassadors*: Two Types of Ambiguity," addresses the question of his ambiguity specifically in this novel. Her argument is much worth revisiting. She begins by distinguishing the "two types." First, there is ambiguity in the "common loose sense of the word ... mean[ing] simply obscure, puzzling, mystifying, baffling, and the like." According to Krook, there is "scarcely a page" in the novel that doesn't exhibit ambiguity in this general sense, and she provides two elliptical passages—exchanges between Strether and Maria, then between Strether and Marie—as evidence that these are "mainly a function of James's late style."[20] The second type, however, has the "more precise meaning" and refers to a text or work in which "everything can be read in two and *only* two ways. The text—meaning every key episode, dialogue, and even utterance—admits of two alternative and contradictory readings, each self-complete and wholly consistent with all the data."[21]

For this second ambiguity, the paradigm case in James is obviously *The Turn of the Screw,* but Krook points out that there are "pockets" of it in a number of James's novels (including some of those I have just alluded to above). Krook does not believe that *The Ambassadors* "as a whole" is ambiguous in this special sense, but she claims there is indeed one great "pocket" of it in the novel: to wit, "Chad's transformation" and his "transvaluation of values vis a vis Woollett." In the remainder of the article, Krook with her usual skill lays out careful textual evidence both for and against interpretations respecting Chad's metamorphosis, and she contends that "there is nothing to tilt the balance decisively in favour of one or the other, thus leaving the ambiguity total and unresolved."[22]

Interestingly, Krook also proposes that the overall novel, despite so much ambiguity of the first kind on almost all pages, is *not* ambiguous in the second special sense. And yet this one great "pocket," the mystery of Chad's transformation, is precisely the crux on which the reliability and legitimacy of Strether's *own* entire transvaluation in the novel seems to depend. Krook herself observes that "a huge question-mark hangs over the validity of Strether's vision";[23] moreover, Strether —in a moment of self-doubt before he reconvinces himself— admits in Book Eighth that if he is wrong about Chad, his own position will "crack and crumble" and he himself will be revealed as "silly" (II, 81).

Krook's broader theme is that all of this "precisely is the design of Jamesian ambiguity: to leave the reader faced with two and only two interpretations of the data, which are mutually exclusive ... yet each of which is wholly consistent with all the available evidence."[24] On the other hand, she does not seem to be suggesting that James's art is a neat trick, a parallel, for example, to Frank Stockton's reader's choice between the lady or the tiger. Rather, her deeper point is that, when as readers we decide our interpretation of Chad, it must be based on "something other than the evidence."

> You can choose, in a word, only by an act of faith—"blind" faith—in the validity and integrity of your own vision. And this is the deep truth about human experience and human knowledge that the Jamesian ambiguity is designed to dramatise. When in life a crucial act of choice has to be made between two and only two possible lines of action ... and the facts or data constituting the evidence are intractably ambiguous in supporting ... *both* of the two and only two alternatives, the crucial choice can only be made by an act of faith.[25]

If we agree to leave aside a third alternative, that Strether himself decisively "re-reconstructs" Chad "downward" in Books Eleventh and Twelfth, a thesis I have proffered in chapters 4 and 6 of this study, Krook's analysis remains most pertinent to the workings of James's ambiguity. First of all, her observation that "a huge question mark hangs over the validity of Strether's vision" is another way, I believe, for us to comprehend the residual presence of negative realism in a text that is otherwise mainly a hymn to positive realism. Second, she analyzes the way Strether convinces and then reconvinces himself of Chad's improvement by invoking either supporters who are anything but objective or else others, like Mamie Pocock, whose conversation does not necessarily mean what Strether concludes it does. This analysis drives home James's powerful gift for dramatizing the psychological phenomenon all of us share in making the case that corresponds to our desires and needs. In short, it underscores James as a great psychological realist.

Third, Krook's thesis that we all choose ultimately by an act of blind faith is one that should evoke for us both Strether's and the novel's existential, or "intrinsic," ethical matrix discussed earlier with the help of Paul B. Armstrong in chapter 5. Furthermore, the same point, that the dilemma of choice in the face of contradictory evidence is inevitably an act of faith, is a view that dovetails profoundly with William James, especially in "The Will to Believe." For there is no more William Jamesian a hero than Strether in his persistent belief in the "high road" of his experience, including, as long as he is able, the belief that Chad is transformed. And even when he *has* been undeceived by experience and is asked by Maria Gostrey at the end what he has to go home to, Strether chooses the positive tack: "There will always be something," he replies, "I shall see what I can make of it" (II, 325). Strether's stance here leads directly to William James once again, especially in "The Will to Believe," when William rhetorically asks the would-be skeptic or "safe" positivist, "Dupery for dupery, what proof is there that dupery through hope is so much worse than dupery through fear?"[26] Strether's tack, nevertheless, also remains compatible with his "melancholy eloquence," much as does William's "tender-mindedness" with his "tough-mindedness" in philosophy, and as Henry James's comic vision does with his tragic sense of life.

9

Conclusion: Sacred Geometry
and Return of the Exile

He has come so far through his total little experience that he has
come out on the other side.

—*Project of Novel* (1900)[1]

In chapter 7, I suggested that *The Ambassadors* is not quite a bona fide
parallel modern epic work despite its interesting feature of possessing
a 12-part structure. Having argued that position, I wish now, however,
to conclude by exploring an idea proposed by Michael Seidel: that this
novel possesses "a plot as old as the dusty hills of Mycenae and the
undulating plains of the Troas, the abduction of Helen by Paris that
sets off the action of the Homeric *Iliad*." That is to say, for James
"Paris is the same lure and threat to the ethos of America that Troy
was for the Greeks."[2] This perspective tends to make Chad into a Helen figure, which may not satisfy some readers, but it also opens up the
novel momentarily, at least, to the surprising idea of Strether as a sort
of reluctant Achilles, a person who refuses to act on behalf of the ag-

grieved society back home. His conversation with Miss Barrace in Book Tenth even resonates vaguely with the Homeric epic. "[I]t all depends on you," Miss Barrace declares. "I don't want to turn the knife in your vitals, but that's naturally what you just now meant by our all being on top of you. We know you as the hero of the drama, and we're gathered to see what you'll do." Strether replies to this assessment: "I think that must be why the hero has taken refuge in this corner. He's scared of his heroism—he shrinks from his part" (II, 179).

Obviously, the differences between Strether and Achilles register as at least as great as, or greater than, any overtones of similarity. For one thing, Achilles's wrath and hubris juxtapose Strether's constant self-abasement and empathy for others—a non-Achaian quality that recalls instead Keats's great concept of negative capability. Furthermore, Achilles eventually does take up arms for the Greeks, whereas Strether does not ultimately throw his weight behind the forces, so to speak, of Woollett. Third and most obviously, Achilles is a great fighter and Strether is an ambassador, although hardly a very successful one, as things turn out.

What makes the topic of Homeric analogue so meaningful, therefore, is not the parallel between such characters as Strether and Chad with Achilles and Helen but something else Seidel squarely puts his finger on: "The intricate and calculated way James combines his comic and epic plots is one of the glories of *The Ambassadors*."[3] James's novel is a world masterpiece because somehow its plot "reattaches" to narrative archetypes in the West. Or rather, it is a world masterpiece because its plot accomplishes this in the face of the book's enormous predominance of individual character, consciousness, and psychological depth—which is its own territory as opposed to the universal archetype with which it nevertheless participates.

One key place at which these two levels intersect is the one raised by James's reflection in the Harper's Scenario cited above—the conception of Strether's "crossing-over" and "coming-out" on the "other side." This is both the journey of the exile—that of Odysseus, if you will, rather than Achilles—and it is also the potential pattern for chiasmus. In one respect, chiasmatic inversion, in some form or another, has been associated with Henry James as long ago as E. M.

Conclusion: Sacred Geometry and Return of the Exile

Forster's discussion back in 1927 of the "hour-glass pattern" of *The Ambassadors*. But Forster's whole point was that James sacrificed human life to an exquisite pattern. Then in 1982 Ralf Norrman argued for the presence of chiasmus throughout James's corpus as a whole. However, while he did not share Forster's cryptic negativity, he did eventually conclude that chiasmus in James was pathological and even paradigmatic of the novelist's intense ambiguity and "insecurity."[4]

In *The Ambassadors,* the most obvious chiasmatic inversion is Strether and Chad's exchange of places, highlighted periodically, as in Book Seventh, when Strether uses all his influence to persuade Chad *not* to return as yet. Moreover, as Seidel points out, "One of the calculated ironies of *The Ambassadors* is that Chad tends to clear out of town just as Strether, in one way or another, moves in."[5] Of course, much of that irony lies in the fact that *both* Chad and Marie are so often away at the same time, and Strether fails to see the connection. As he reflects to himself in a different context, his "usual case" was that "he was for ever missing things through his general genius for missing them, while others were for ever picking them up through a contrary bent" (II, 185–86). This conception, too, borders on the chiasmatic. When he does come across the couple at Cheval Blanc in Book Eleventh, he finds that Chad has replaced him literally in Mme. de Vionnet's metaphorical boat. And yet his own corollary to his self-confessed failure just quoted can apply to Cheval Blanc equally well: "And it was others who looked abstemious and he who looked greedy; it was he somehow who finally paid, and it was others who mainly partook" (II, 186). Just as chiasmus with Strether centers first in his exchange with Chad yet opens outward and recapitulates itself in other contexts, so other characters, too, appear to share in it: Europeanized American Maria Gostrey gets partly re-Americanized by her attraction for a newly Europeanized Strether; little Bilham, another Europeanized American, can begin, at least, to become re-Americanized by his association with Mamie; Waymarsh, who is floundering abroad, gets powerfully re-Americanized by the new American ambassador Sarah Pocock.

All these examples suggest that chiasmus is a "crossing over" of national boundaries and thus an avenue into James's internationalism and cultural analysis. Such crossings, moreover, make of the characters, Strether above all, figures of exile. Seidel points acutely to the "tension" that "marks the design of the novel, its local obligations and international longings."[6] That exact tension, of course, belongs to the other Homeric figure Odysseus, whom Poe, in his poem "To Helen," depicts borne along in a boat in somewhat Strether-like terms: "The weary, way-worn wanderer bore/To his own native shore." Like that of Odysseus, Strether's return home is highly charged and richly complicated, but in James the richness and the complication express themselves through chiasmus. When the exile returns, he is as much a pilgrim newly arrived on his "native shore" as in his journey away from it. Refamiliarization expresses a dynamic as great as does the discovery of brand-new lands or ideas, perhaps an even greater one in that it more fully completes the process and incorporates new discovery into its broader experience. This idea is clearly what Wordsworth expounds in his "Intimations Ode" and also T. S. Eliot in his famous conclusion to *Four Quartets,* when he writes that "the end of all our exploring/Will be to arrive where we started/And know the place for the first time."

Odysseus has to return to his house as a beggar in order to reappropriate with authenticity his "native shore." Strether too—unless we object to his decline of Maria's offer as too "abstemious"—has to return from his exile as a beggar in the sense of having forsworn all his advantages with Mrs. Newsome. Doubtless this is what Maria has in mind when she asks, "To what do you go home?" Strether admits, "I don't know. There will always be something." Maria tries to identify that something: "To a great difference," she calls it while keeping hold of the hand Strether extends to her in farewell. "A great difference—no doubt," he admits. "Yet I shall see what I can make of it" (II, 325).

It is not necessary that we interpret Strether's return as an exile to mean that, like Odysseus, he will ultimately have all things restored to him. For we have already seen that *The Ambassadors* is a tragicomedy, whereas *The Odyssey* is a comedy and *The Iliad* a tragedy. What Strether's exchange with Maria does hold out, however, is the promise of the "difference" attending the reentry back into the familiar. Seidel argues most persuasively that James's situation during his own return visit to America late in life and recorded in *The American Scene* (1907) is very much the same as Strether's return home at the end of *The Ambassadors*. That parallel reinforces our sense on still other grounds of the unusually close ties between Strether and James. Strether, we recall, in the same conversation with Maria, compares his "recent history" to the figure on "the old clock at Berne," who "jigged" out in "the public eye" and went in "on the other side" (II, 322); James speaks of his protagonist in the Scenario as having "come so far" as to "come out on the other side." Strether's clock-figure metaphor for himself is "in character," that is, somewhat self-deprecatory, whereas James's for Strether in the Scenario has the pattern of chiasmus embedded within it. And yet these two images that end with "the other side" and that suggest circular inversion are compatible. And compatible with them both is James's high regard for this novel as exhibiting a "superior roundness."

In these troubled times, it is at least possible once again to associate chiasmus with the "sacred geometry," as in the past when it was found in certain branches of Hermetic literature and thought. Its newer currency today derives from the connections some have seen between chiasmus and the double helix, in other words, from the deep structure of life. We do not need to read James-Strether as a profound spiritual seer, although one critic alone and without support does read the novel that way.[7] What can and should be said, at least, is that the Jamesian geometry is in no wise an antithesis of human life, as E. M. Forster believed, but a more comprehensive expression of it; nor is it, moreover, a persistent mark of pathology or insecurity, as Norrman contends. Most important, its presence in James does not diminish the psychologist, the pragmatist, or the historian of consciousness. From another point of view, chiasmus can indeed transpose into polarity— and polarity rightly understood as a positive interrelationship of opposition and, in Coleridgean terms, the fundamental law of life. One reason chiasmus in James translates into polarity rather than pragmatism, for instance, is that it is the *universalizing* principle of the imagination to which James's individual art can be referred. Pragmatism, we recall, captures best the *individualizing* art itself. Seidel in his own way senses this sort of issue when he writes that "James's adaptation of traditional plots, melding nationally and socially determined obligations with the finer tuning of individual consciousness, [is what] gives his work real dimension."[8]

Henry James's geometry, then, provides added depth to his already acknowledged mastery of the international novel. It also allows us to approach the other kinds of patterns distinctive to his art that his best critics have unearthed over decades of attention. For example, it is at once deeply human, unendingly ironic, and ultimately a pattern to be cherished that *The Ambassadors* is a bildungsroman, an initiation novel, but one with a middle-aged protagonist rather than, as the handbooks say, "a sensitive young person" who comes to learn about life. Another example: James's geometry must surely enable us to appreciate anew R. P. Blackmur's thesis in "The Loose and Baggy Monsters" that James's later work always reveals a profoundly classic form undergirding the convolutions of idiom and complex systems of narrative indirection. If the student who reads this study comprehends only the implication of the Blackmur thesis for *The Ambassadors,* I believe that student already has become a good reader of the late James.

Finally, however, when we move from the universal back to the particularity of James's genius in *The Ambassadors,* we find that once again he has constructed a "true dialectical inquiry,"[9] as always in his best fiction, from *Daisy Miller* to *The Golden Bowl.* That is, he looks all around his subject and fulfills his goal expressed in "The Art of Fiction" to "try to be one on whom nothing is lost."[10] Instead of seeing his subject from a single side he embraces the plurality, flux, and multiplicity of aspects in order to shape artistic unity out of them all—a far greater challenge than any single-sided theme. This trait has shown itself wherever we have touched the novel throughout this study but nowhere more than in its germ, which James insisted contained "[t]he whole case" of the book in miniature.[11]

James ventures in his New York preface to say that Strether's irrepressible outburst to little Bilham could even be "the voice of the false position."[12] That assessment can at once open up the novel for a critique of Strether by a certain kind of critic so disposed. Yet it equally permits an empathetic approach to him by a very different-minded critic, since a "false position" for an empathetic critic, is still the human one; besides, the "false position" resides more or less halfway through Strether's adventure in Book Fifth and does not necessarily mean to characterize the ending—where the first critic, so to speak, already awaits and says it does. Of such is James's "dialectical inquiry."

These opposing critical positions have solid enough Jamesian justification: the first has the continuity of Strether's deepest unyielding "temperament," his Emersonian "Lord of Life." The second has James's commitment to a dynamic central character, one who grows, who can even have a bildungsroman experience in middle age, and who lives in a William Jamesian world where things are never static but always "in the making." The same dialectic is present when James in the preface speaks of Strether's outburst as "melancholy eloquence."[13] By marrying a comedy of manners to an elegiac protagonist whose interior consciousness carries the point of view, the novel continues to weave its fluctuating perspectives, its unforeseen loyalties, decisions, and emotional heartaches. And yet the weaving itself, however provisional the theme of its design, remains astonishingly unified.

Notes and References

Chapter One

1. James's high praise for *The Ambassadors* can be found in Henry James, *Literary Criticism: French Writers, Other Europeans Writers, the Prefaces to the New York Edition,* ed. Leon Edel and Mark Wilson (New York: Library of America, 1984), 1306; the term "major phase" was first used by F. O. Matthiessen in his landmark study *Henry James: The Major Phase* (New York: Oxford University Press, 1944).

2. Daniel M. Fogel, *"Daisy Miller": A Dark Comedy of Manners* (Boston: Twayne Publishers, 1990), 3.

3. See James's critical biography *Hawthorne* (1879), in *Literary Criticism: Essays on Literature, American Writers, English Writers,* ed. Leon Edel and Mark Wilson (New York: Library of America), 319–457, 458–74; also Robert Emmet Long, *The Great Extension: Henry James and the Legacy of Hawthorne* (Pittsburgh: University of Pittsburgh Press, 1979); and Richard Broadhead, *The School of Hawthorne* (New York: Oxford University Press, 1986).

4. See especially Sergio Perosa, *Henry James and the Experimental Novel* (Charlottesville: University Press of Virginia, 1978), and Walter Isle, *Experiments in Form: Henry James's Novels, 1896–1901* (Cambridge, Mass.: Harvard University Press, 1968).

5. Fogel, *"Daisy Miller,"* 5.

6. For James's influence on modernism see John Carlos Rowe, *The Theoretical Dimensions of Henry James* (Madison: University of Wisconsin Press, 1984). For his specific influence on modern poetry see David Perkins, *A History of Modern Poetry: From the 1890s to Pound, Eliot, and Yeats* (Cambridge, Mass.: Harvard University Press, 1976). For discusssions of James and Conrad see Paul B. Armstrong, *The Challenge of Bewilderment: Understanding and Representation in James, Conrad, and Ford* (Ithaca: Cornell University

Press, 1987), and Elsa Nettles, *James and Conrad* (Athens: University of Georgia Press, 1977). For a discussion of James, Joyce, and Woolf see Daniel M. Fogel, *Covert Relations: James Joyce, Virginia Woolf, and Henry James* (Charlottesville: University Press of Virginia, 1990).

7. Joseph Conrad, "An Appreciation" (1905), in *Henry James: A Collection of Critical Essays,* ed. Leon Edel (Englewood Cliffs, N.J.: Prentice-Hall, 1963), 15.

8. R. P. Blackmur, *Literary History of the United States,* ed. Robert E. Spiller et al. (New York: The MacMillan Co., 1953), 1039.

9. Ezra Pound, "Brief Note," *Little Review* (August 1918): 7–9; T. S. Eliot, "A Prediction," in *Henry James: A Collection of Critical Essays,* ed. Leon Edel, 56.

10. See Stephen Spender, *The Destructive Element: A Study of Modern Writers and Beliefs* (Boston: Houghton Mifflin, 1936); Lionel Trilling, *The Liberal Imagination* (New York: Macmillan, 1948); and David A. Leeming, "An Interview with James Baldwin on Henry James," *Henry James Review* 8 (1986–87): 47–56.

11. James, *The Complete Notebooks of Henry James,* ed. Leon Edel and Lyall H. Powers (New York: Oxford University Press, 1987), 141.

12. James, *Letters: 1895–1916,* vol. 4, ed. Leon Edel (Cambridge, Mass.: Harvard University Press, 1984), 160; and James, *Literary Criticism: Prefaces,* 1305.

Chapter Two

1. Henry James, *Literary Criticism: Prefaces,* 1080.

2. James, *The Ambassadors,* vol. I (New York: Charles Scribner's Sons, 1909), 218. This text is the New York Edition, which also comprises vols. XXI and XXII of *The Novels and Tales of Henry James.* All references to *The Ambassadors* are to this edition and are cited hereafter parenthetically in my text as volume I or II.

3. See chapter 1, note 12.

4. For a more thorough study of the genesis of James's composition of *The Ambassadors* see Richard A. Hocks, "Quite the Best, 'All Round,' of All My Productions: The Multiple Versions of the Jamesian Germ for 'The Ambassadors,' " in *Biographies of Books,* ed. James Barbour and Tom Quirk (Columbia: University of Missouri Press, 1996), 110–30.

5. R. P. Blackmur, "The Loose and Baggy Monsters of Henry James" (1951), in *Studies in Henry James,* ed. Veronica A. Makowsky (New York: New Directions, 1983), 125–46. This seminal essay originally appeared in *Accent* 11 (1951): 129–46.

Notes and References

Chapter Three

1. Early examples of each position are Oliver Elton, "The Novels of Mr. Henry James," *Quarterly Review,* vol. 198 (October 1903): 358–79; F. T. Cooper, "The Novelist's Omniscience and Some Recent Books," *Bookman,* vol. 18 (January 1904): 530–37; and Joseph Conrad, "An Appreciation," *North American Review,* vol. 180 (January 1905): 102–8. Critical of James's obscurity and other of his techniques are F. M. Colby, "In Darkest James," *Bookman,* vol. 16 (November 1902): 259–60; W. C. Brownell, "Henry James," *Atlantic Monthly,* vol. 95 (April 1905): 496–519; and H. G. Wells, *Boon* (London: Fisher Unwin, 1915).

2. Mrs. Humphrey Ward, *A Writer's Recollections* (London: Collins, 1918), 336.

3. T. S. Eliot, "In Memory" and "The Hawthorne Aspect," *Little Review* (August 1918): 45.

4. Joseph Warren Beach, *The Method of Henry James* (New Haven: Yale University Press, 1918), 155.

5. Percy Lubbock, *The Craft of Fiction* (New York: Scribner's, 1921), 156, 171.

6. Van Wyck Brooks, *The Pilgrimage of Henry James* (New York: E. P. Dutton, 1925), 140.

7. Vernon Louis Parrington, *The Beginnings of Critical Realism in America: 1860–1920* (New York: Harcourt, Brace and World, 1920), 241.

8. E. M. Forster, *Aspects of the Novel* (New York: Harcourt, Brace and World, 1927), 219, 228.

9. Maxwell Geismar, *Henry James and the Jacobites* (New York: Hill and Wang, 1962). Geismar's English title was *Henry James and his Cult.*

10. R. P. Blackmur, introduction to *The Art of the Novel: Critical Prefaces by Henry James,* vii–xxix (New York: Scribner's, 1934); see also Cornelia P. Kelley, *The Early Development of Henry James* (Urbana: University of Illinois Press, 1930), and Constance Rourke, *Native American Humor: A Study of the National Character* (New York: Harcourt Brace Jovanovich, 1931).

11. Lincoln Kirstein, Yvor Winters, and Allen Tate, eds., "Homage to Henry James," *Hound and Horn* 7 (1934): 361–562 (special issue).

12. Graham Greene, "The Private Universe" (1936), in *Collection of Critical Essays,* ed. Leon Edel, 111; F. O. Matthiessen, *Major Phase,* 18–41.

13. Matthiessen, *Major Phase,* 40.

14. Leon Edel, *Henry James: The Untried Years, 1843–1870; The Conquest of London, 1870–1881; The Middle Years, 1882–1895; The Treacherous Years, 1895–1901; The Master, 1901–1916* (Philadelphia: J. B. Lippincott,

1953, 1962, 1969, 1972); J. A. Ward, *The Imagination of Disaster: Evil in the Fiction of Henry James* (Lincoln: University of Nebraska Press, 1961); Sallie Sears, *The Negative Imagination: Form and Perspective in the Novels of Henry James* (Ithaca: Cornell University Press, 1968).

15. Christof Wegelin, "The Lesson of Social Beauty," *The Image of Europe in Henry James* (Dallas: Southern Methodist University Press, 1958), 86–121.

16. Ian Watt, "The First Paragraph of *The Ambassadors:* An Explication," *Essays in Criticism* X (July 1960): 274.

17. Ruth B. Yeazell, *Language and Knowledge in the Late Novels of Henry James* (Chicago: University of Chicago Press, 1976); Robert L. Gale, *The Caught Image: Figurative Language in the Fiction of Henry James* (Chapel Hill: University of North Carolina Press, 1964).

18. Sergio Perosa, *Experimental Novel*, 203.

19. Nicola Bradbury, *Henry James: The Later Novels* (New York: Oxford University Press, 1979), 69–71.

20. Henry James, *Literary Criticism: Prefaces*, 1313.

21. Richard A. Hocks, "The Several Canons of Henry James," *American Literary Realism 1870–1910* 23 (Spring 1991): 68–81.

22. For a reader-response successor to Lubbock, in effect, see Wayne C. Booth, *The Rhetoric of Fiction* (Chicago: University of Chicago Press, 1961), 339–74.

23. Sarah B. Daugherty, *The Literary Criticism of Henry James* (Athens: Ohio University Press, 1981); Daniel M. Fogel, *Henry James and the Structure of the Romantic Imagination* (Baton Rouge: Louisiana State University Press, 1981), 23–48.

24. Bradbury, *An Annotated Critical Bibliography of Henry James* (New York: St. Martin's Press, 1987), 3.

25. John Carlos Rowe, *Theoretical Dimensions*, 256–57.

26. Mark Seltzer, *Henry James and the Art of Power* (Ithaca: Cornell University Press, 1984); Elizabeth Allen, *A Woman's Place in the Novels of Henry James* (London: Macmillan, 1984); Virginia Fowler, *Henry James's American Girl: The Embroidery on the Canvas* (Madison: University of Wisconsin Press, 1984).

27. Marcia Jacobson, *Henry James and the Mass Market* (University: University of Alabama Press, 1983); Anne T. Margolis, *Henry James and the Problem of Audience* (Ann Arbor: UMI Research Press, 1985); Michael Anesko, *'Friction with the Market': Henry James and the Profession of Authorship* (New York: Oxford University Press, 1968).

28. Donna Przybylowicz, *Desire and Repression: The Dialectic of Self and Other in the Late Works of Henry James* (University: University of Alabama Press, 1986). For examples of William Veeder's post-Freudian analysis

see Veeder, "The Portrait of a Lack," in *New Essays on "The Portrait of a Lady,"* ed. Joel Porte (New York: Cambridge University Press, 1990), 95–121, and "Toxic Mothers, Cultural Criticism: 'In the Cage' and Elsewhere," *The Henry James Review* 14 (Fall 1993): 264–72. For Ash's post-Freudian approach see Beth Sharon Ash, "Narcissism and the Gilded Image: A Psychoanalytic Reading of *The Golden Bowl,*" *The Henry James Review* 15 (Winter 1994): 55–90.

29. Paul B. Armstrong, "Reality and/or Interpretation in *The Ambassadors,*" in *Challenge of Bewilderment,* 63–106.

30. Alfred Habegger, *Henry James and the "Woman Business"* (New York: Cambridge University Press, 1989).

31. David McWhirter, *Desire and Love in Henry James: A Study of the Late Novels* (Cambridge, England: Cambridge University Press, 1989), 13–82.

32. Adeline R. Tintner, *The Museum World of Henry James* (Ann Arbor: UMI Research Press, 1986); *The Book World of Henry James: Appropriating the Classics* (Ann Arbor: UMI Research Press, 1987); *The Pop World of Henry James: From Fairy Tales to Science Fiction* (Ann Arbor, Mich.: UMI Research Press, 1989); *The Cosmopolitan World of Henry James: An Intertextual Study* (Baton Rouge: Louisiana State University Press, 1991); *Henry James and the Lust of the Eyes: Thirteen Artists in his Work* (Baton Rouge: Louisiana State University Press, 1993); Tintner and Leon Edel, *The Library of Henry James* (Ann Arbor, Mich.: UMI Research Press, 1987).

33. Daniel M. Fogel, *Covert Relations,* 42–43, 24–25, 144–45, 117–18.

34. Philip Horne, *Henry James and Revision: The New York Edition* (New York: Oxford University Press, 1990). See also David McWhirter, ed., *Henry James's New York Edition: The Construction of Authorship* (Stanford: Stanford University Press, 1995).

35. Susan M. Griffin, *The Historical Eye: The Texture of the Visual in Late James* (Boston: Northeastern University Press, 1991); Ross Posnock, *The Trial of Curiosity: Henry James, William James, and the Challenge of Modernity* (New York: Oxford University Press, 1991), vii, 293.

36. Priscilla L. Walton, *The Disruption of the Feminine in Henry James* (Toronto: University of Toronto Press, 1992); Mary Cross, *Henry James: The Contingencies of Style* (New York: St. Martin's Press, 1993); Paul G. Beidler, *Frames in James: "The Tragic Muse," "The Turn of the Screw," "What Maisie Knew" and "The Ambassadors"* (Victoria, B.C.: University of Victoria Press, 1993); Julie Rivkin, "The Logic of Delegation in *The Ambassadors,*" *PMLA* 101 (October 1986): 819–31.

37. Kelly Cannon, *Henry James and Masculinity* (New York: St. Martin's Press, 1994); Kenneth Warren, *Black and White Strangers: Race and*

American Literary Realism (Chicago: University of Chicago Press, 1993), 103–4.

38. Carol Holly, *Intensely Family: The Inheritance of Family Shame and the Autobiographies of Henry James* (Madison: University of Wisconsin Press, 1995); Paul John Eakin, "Henry James's 'Obscure Hurt': Can Autobiography Serve Biography?" *New Literary History* 19 (1988): 675–92.

39. Richard A. Hocks, *Henry James and Pragmatistic Thought* (Chapel Hill: University of North Carolina, 1974); Stephen Donadio, *Nietzsche, Henry James, and the Artistic Will* (New York: Oxford University. Press, 1978); Armstrong, *The Phenomenology of Henry James* (Chapel Hill: University of North Carolina Press, 1983); Merle A. Williams, *Henry James and the Philosophical Novel: Being and Seeing* (Cambridge, England: Cambridge University Press, 1993).

40. G. L. Hagberg recently adds to the literature on James and philosophy in *Meaning and Interpretation: Wittgenstein, Henry James, and Literary Knowledge* (Ithaca: Cornell University Press, 1994); however, he does not deal with any of James's novels or even any tales written during the major phase.

41. The first major new biography of James since Edel's is Fred Kaplan, *Henry James: The Imagination of Genius* (New York: William Morrow, 1992); the new superbly edited correspondence between the brothers is *The Correspondence of William James, Vols. I–III: William and Henry*, ed. Ignas K. Skrupskelis and Elizabeth M. Berkeley (Charlottesville: University Press of Virginia, 1992, 1993, 1994).

42. Henry James, "The Art of Fiction," in *Literary Criticism: Essays on Literature*, ed. Edel and Wilson, 54.

43. Ross Posnock, "Henry James and the Limits of Historicism," *The Henry James Review* 16 (Fall 1995): 274.

44. Philip Fisher, *Redrawing the Boundaries: The Transformation of English and American Literary Studies*, ed. Stephen Greenblatt and Giles Gunn (New York: Modern Languages Association, 1992), 235.

45. Two helpful recent guides for students of James are Robert L. Gale, *A Henry James Encyclopedia* (Westport, Conn.: Greenwood Press, 1989), and *A Companion to Henry James*, ed. Daniel M. Fogel (Westport, Conn.: Greenwood Press, 1993).

Chapter Four

1. See Robert L. Gale, *Encyclopedia*, 16.

2. Henry James, *Literary Criticism: Prefaces*, 1313.

3. Ibid.

4. Ibid., 1315.

5. Ibid., 1316.

6. Percy Lubbock, *The Craft of Fiction*, 156–202 and passim.

Notes and References

7. Strictly speaking there are more "scenes" in *The Ambassadors* than "pictures"; of the 36 chapters in the novel, 13 use scene exclusively, 19 mix the two, and 4 use picture alone. Yet the effect is utterly unlike that in *The Awkward Age,* for instance, which reads almost like a play. Picture, which gives a "third dimension" to James's world, is somewhat analogous to the shading treatment in Michelangelo's drawings and also prominent in the Sistine Chapel ceiling before the recent cleaning of the fresco.

8. Henry James, *The Portrait of a Lady,* ed. Robert D. Bamberg (New York: W. W. Norton, 1975), 489.

9. For an excellent discussion of James's English "anxiety of influence" with regard to Trollope, see John Carlos Rowe, *Theoretical Dimensions,* 58–83.

10. Henry James, "The Art of Fiction," in *Literary Criticism: Essays on Literature,* ed. Edel and Wilson, 46–47.

11. See Alan W. Bellringer, *The Ambassadors* (London: George Allen and Unwin, 1984), 46–47.

12. James, *Literary Criticism: Prefaces,* 1317.

13. James, "The Art of Fiction," in *Literary Criticism: Essays on Literature,* ed. Edel and Wilson, 52–53.

Chapter Five

1. See Alan W. Bellringer, *The Ambassadors,* 48. For the "house of fiction" conceit see Henry James, *Literary Criticism: Prefaces,* 1075.

2. James, *Literary Criticism: Prefaces,* 1130–31.

3. Ibid., 1041.

4. For a discussion of Isabel in relation to Daisy see Richard A. Hocks, "*Daisy Miller,* Backward into the Past: A Centennial Essay," *The Henry James Review* I, 2 (Winter 1980): 164–67.

5. For a discussion of James and polarity see especially Hocks, *Pragmatistic Thought,* 152–81 and passim; also Daniel M. Fogel, *Structure of Romantic Imagination,* 23–48 and passim. Polarity in *The Ambassadors* is addressed in chapter 7.

6. James, *Henry James Letters,* vol. III, ed. Leon Edel (Cambridge, Mass.: Harvard University Press, 1980), 499.

7. James, *Literary Criticism: Prefaces,* 1269–91. See also Bellringer, *The Ambassadors,* 12–13.

8. Ian Watt, in "The First Paragraph," 270–74, discusses the novel as a series of "questions" taken from its opening phrase, "Strether's first question."

9. Hocks, "A Centennial Essay," 178. For some of my profile on Mamie and Jeanne I am indebted to Dorothea Krook, *Henry James's "The Ambassadors": A Critical Study* (New York: AMS Press, Inc., 1996), 79–83.

10. Christof Wegelin, "The Lesson of Social Beauty," 88.

11. Ibid.

12. Ibid., 90.

13. For a discussion of this specifically Kantian moral perspective in James, see William H. Gass, "The High Brutality of Good Intentions," *Accent* 18 (1958): 62–71; for extensive discussions of the same moral faculty in less purely Kantian terms, see Richard A. Hocks, *Henry James: A Study of the Short Fiction* (Boston: Twayne Publishers, 1990), 61–69, 91–105, and Hocks, *Pragmatistic Thought,* 134–51. My discussions above focus on James's tales "The Pupil" (1891) and "A Round of Visits" (1910) and on his novel *The Spoils of Poynton* (1897).

14. This chapter is from Paul B. Armstrong, *The Challenge of Bewilderment,* 63–105.

15. Ibid., 94.

16. Ibid., 64.

17. Ibid., 67.

18. Ibid., 70.

19. Ibid., 64. Opposed to Armstrong's—and many others'—thesis regarding James and consciousness is Sharon Cameron, *Thinking in Henry James* (Chicago: University of Chicago Press, 1989). Cameron claims, pace James himself in *Literary Criticism: Prefaces* and elsewhere, that consciousness in James is not to be identified with psychology—anyone's psychology.

20. Armstrong, *The Challenge of Bewilderment,* 65.

21. Ibid., 79.

22. Ibid., 92. Compare this formulation with Hocks, *Pragmatistic Thought,* 63: "Strether actively and radically meets the discovery [at Cheval Blanc]; he enters into a reciprocal relation with it, grafting meaning while receiving in kind; he empties every possible insight about himself, his previous assumptions, the thoughts of the two lovers in having to deal with *him,* and even the imagined responses of those back at Paris, into it." I shall return to this statement and this issue in the next chapter.

23. Armstrong, *The Challenge of Bewilderment,* 99, 101.

24. Ibid., 101.

25. Ibid., 105.

Chapter Six

1. Henry James, "Hawthorne," in *The Shock of Recognition: The Development of Literature in the United States Recorded by the Men Who Made It,* ed. Edmund Wilson (New York: The Modern Library, 1943), 476.

2. T. S. Eliot, "Henry James," in ibid., 861.

3. Ibid., 856.

4. See chapter 3, notes 41 and 42. This is a relatively small segment from a very large body of philosophical scholarship.

5. Alan W. Bellringer, *The Ambassadors,* 21–31. For a discussion of James's moral and cultural themes along Arnoldian lines see also Alwyn Berland, *Culture and Conduct in the Novels of Henry James* (Cambridge, England: Cambridge University Press, 1981).

6. Bellringer, *The Ambassadors,* 24.

7. Berland, *Culture and Conduct,* 28–37.

8. Bellringer, *The Ambassadors,* 25.

9. Susan M. Griffin, "The Selfish Eye: Strether's Principles of Psychology," in Griffin, *The Historical Eye,* 33.

10. Ibid., 33; see also corroborating evidence, 54.

11. Ibid.

12. Ibid., 40.

13. Ibid., 43, 44.

14. Ibid., 37, 42.

15. Richard A. Hocks, *Pragmatistic Thought,* 63.

16. F. O. Matthiessen, *The James Family: Including Selections from the Writings of Henry James, Senior, William, Henry, and Alice James* (New York: Alfred A. Knopf, 1961), 334. A superb exposition of the *Principles of Psychology* as a literary masterpiece can be found in Jacques Barzun, *A Stroll with William James* (New York: Harper & Row, 1983), 34–82; Barzun's beautifully written study takes a viewpoint on William and Henry's work that is congenial with this study and my *Pragmatistic Thought.*

17. William James, *The Principles of Psychology,* vol. I (New York: Henry Holt and Co., 1890), 243.

18. See also Hocks, *Pragmatistic Thought,* 33–34.

19. Matthiessen, *The James Family,* 234. "Most of it is quite unreadable," William writes to Henry, "but you may find some pages in the second volume that will go. Also the earlier pages of the chapter on Consciousness of Self."

20. Matthiessen, *The James Family,* 343.

21. One reason many critics and scholars beginning with Matthiessen and Ralph Barton Perry have misread or misunderstood Henry's avowal of pragmatism and reference to Molière is that William repeatedly takes issue with Henry's late style in their correspondence. Nevertheless, for a closer look at William's qualifications of, even ambiguity in, his objections, together with the abrupt cessation of such criticism after Henry's avowals of apposition, see Hocks, *Pragmatistic Thought,* esp. 17–26.

22. Matthiessen, *The James Family,* 344.

23. Ibid., 344–45. Matthiessen, who prints this and the two preceding letters to William, says that "HJ [*sic*] declared again that he had embraced pragmatism, without ever making clear quite what he implied thereby." Leon Edel, who in his biography argues a fierce, psychic "Jacob/Esau rivalry" between the two brothers, chooses not to print either the "Pluralistic Universe" or "Meaning of Truth" letter in *Henry James Letters: 1895–16,* ed. Leon Edel, vol. IV (Cambridge, Mass.: Harvard University Press, 1984). Alan W. Bellringer in his monograph on *The Ambassadors,* 38–39, says that "By the time of these letters, James's major novels had been written several years back, however. The application of pragmatism to them has to be examined with the benefit of hindsight."

24. Matthiessen, *The James Family,* 345.

25. This discussion of the embodiment of William James in *The Ambassadors* does not provide the fullest of citations and passages from William James as such. Those wishing to examine such references can do so in my *Pragmatistic Thought,* 38–112 and passim.

26. Such passages inspire Wegelin in *Image of Europe,* 92, 96, 101, to propose that Strether has "quite simply become a pragmatist." My chief difficulty with this claim has been the word "simply." Yet Wegelin does connect Strether's openness to a pragmatic cast of mind.

27. William James, *Principles,* vol. I, 234.

28. William James, *The Meaning of Truth: A Sequel to "Pragmatism"* (New York: Longmans, Green, and Co., 1909), 138, 139.

29. Ibid., 140.

30. William James, *Some Problems of Philosophy: A Beginning of an Introduction to Philosophy* (New York: Longmans, Green, and Co., 1911), 147. Emphasis in the original.

31. James, *The Meaning of Truth,* xii–xiii.

32. James, *Pragmatism: A New Name for Some Old Ways of Thinking* (New York: Longmans, Green, and Co., 1907), 201.

Chapter Seven

1. James, *Notebooks,* 575–76.

2. The great Van Eyck canvas was bought in Brussels in 1815 by Major General James Hay and brought to England; it was exhibited at the British Institution in 1841 and purchased by the National Gallery in 1842, where it still hangs today. See "Early Netherlandish School," in *National Gallery Catalogues,* 2nd ed., revised (London: William Clowes & Sons Ltd., 1955), 39.

3. Henry James, "Gustave Flaubert" (1903), in *Literary Criticism: Prefaces,* ed. Edel and Wilson, 325. A recent interpretation of *The Ambassadors* by way of its origins in French literature is Pierre A. Walker, *Reading Henry James in French Cultural Contexts* (De Kalb: Northern Illinois University Press, 1995), 57–88.

4. In addition to what was said earlier, another excellent place to explore James's connection to modernist poetry is Hugh Kenner, *The Pound Era* (Berkeley: University of California Press, 1971).

5. F. O. Matthiessen, *The Major Phase,* 19.

6. Henry James, *The Letters of Henry James,* ed. Percy Lubbock (New York: Charles Scribner's Sons, 1920), 405.

7. Daniel M. Fogel, *Romantic Imagination,* 38.

8. Ibid., 44.

9. Ibid., 48.

10. William James, *Pragmatism,* 257.

11. Cited by Reginald Abbot in "The Incredible Floating Man: Henry James's Lambert Strether," *The Henry James Review* 11:3 (1990): 177; see also James N. Wise, "The Floating World of Lambert Strether," *Arlington Quarterly* 2 (1969): 80–110.

12. James, *Literary Criticism: Prefaces,* 1084.

13. The conceptual explanations of Coleridgean polarity that follow are derived from Owen Barfield in *What Coleridge Thought* (Middletown, Conn: Wesleyan University Press, 1971); *Speaker's Meaning* (Middletown, Conn.: Wesleyan University Press, 1967), esp. 38–39; and Hocks, *Pragmatistic Thought,* 3–14, 115–20, 173–81.

14. Rene Wellek, "Henry James's Literary Theory and Criticism," *American Literature* 30 (1958): 321.

15. James, "The Art of Fiction," in *Literary Criticism: Essays on Literature,* ed. Edel and Wilson, 54, 59–60.

16. Blackmur, *Literary History of the United States,* 1039.

17. Fogel, *Romantic Imagination,* 33, 37.

18. James, *Literary Criticism: Prefaces,* 1084.

Chapter Eight

1. Henry James, *Notebooks,* 141.

2. Ibid., 564.

3. Daniel M. Fogel, *Dark Comedy of Manners,* 97.

4. Fogel, *Structure of Romantic Imagination,* 43.

5. Krook, *Henry James's "The Ambassadors,"* 101–5.

6. James, *Literary Criticism: Prefaces,* 1305.

7. James, The Art of Fiction," in *Literary Criticism: Essays on Literature,* ed. Edel and Wilson, 46

8. An example of contemporary French theory's dismissal of realism in James is Priscilla L. Walton, *The Disruption of the Feminine in Henry James* (Toronto: University of Toronto Press, 1992).

9. James, *Literary Criticism: Prefaces,* 1057, 1062–63.

10. Ibid., 1063.

11. Compare the more modest extent of the "Textual Notes" representing James's changes in *The Ambassadors,* ed. S. P. Rosenbaum (New York: W. W. Norton, 1994), 348–54, with that of the more substantial "Textual Variants" in *The Wings of the Dove,* ed. J. Donald Crowley and Richard A. Hocks (New York: W. W. Norton, 1978), 423–36.

12. James, *Literary Criticism: Prefaces,* 1332.

13. Ibid., 1337.

14. James, *The American,* ed. Roy Harvey Pearce and Matthew J. Bruccoli (Boston: Houghton Mifflin Co., 1962), 35.

15. James, *Literary Criticism: Prefaces,* 1304, 1306.

16. Ibid., 1053.

17. My entire discussion of *The American* inadvertently yet perhaps inevitably presents the earlier novel as a failure vis-à-vis *The Ambassadors.* An excellent corrective to that view of *The American* is *New Essays on The American,* ed. Martha Banta (New York: Cambridge University Press, 1987). Complementing Banta's fine introduction are contributors Peter Brooks, John Carlos Rowe, Carolyn Porter, and Mark Seltzer.

18. Charles T. Samuels, *The Ambiguity of Henry James* (Urbana: University of Illinois Press, 1971); Edmund Wilson, "The Ambiguity of Henry James," in *The Triple Thinkers* (New York: Oxford University Press, 1948), 88–132.

19. See Wayne C. Booth, *The Rhetoric of Fiction,* 339–74.

20. Dorothea Krook, *"The Ambassadors:* Two Types of Ambiguity," *Neophilologus* 74:1 (1990): 148–50.

21. Ibid., 151.

22. Ibid.

23. Ibid., 154.

24. Ibid.

25. Ibid., 154–55.

26. William James, "The Will to Believe," in *Essays on Faith and Morals* (New York: World Publishing Co., 1962), 58.

Conclusion

1. Henry James, *Notebooks,* 575.

2. Michael Seidel, *Exile and the Narrative Imagination* (New Haven: Yale University Press, 1986), 137.

3. Ibid., 140.

4. Ralf Norrman, *The Insecure World of Henry James: Intensity and Ambiguity* (New York: St. Martin's Press, 1982).

5. Seidel, *Exile,* 154.

6. Ibid., 145.

7. Courtney Johnson Jr., *Henry James and the Evolution of Consciousness: A Study of "The Ambassadors"* (East Lansing: Michigan State University Press, 1987).

8. Seidel, *Exile,* 141.

9. Richard A. Hocks, "A Centennial Essay," 178.

10. James, "The Art of Fiction," in *Literary Criticism :Essays on Literature,* ed. Edel and Wilson, 53.

11. James, *Literary Criticism: Prefaces,* 1304.

12. Ibid., 1309.

13. Ibid., 1305.

Selected Bibliography

Primary Works
Editions of *The Ambassadors*

"The Ambassadors." *North American Review* 176 (January–June 1903): 138–60, 297–320, 459–80, 634–56, 792–816, 945–68; 177 (July–December 1903): 138–60, 297–320, 457–80, 615–40, 779–800, 947–68. The original publication.

The Ambassadors. London: Methuen, September 1903. The first English edition, revised from the magazine publication.

The Ambassadors. New York: Harper & Brothers, 1903. The first American edition, revised from the magazine publication and English edition.

The Ambassadors. Vols. 21 and 22 of *The Novels and Tales of Henry James*. New York: Charles Scribner's Sons, 1909. The New York Edition, which comprises James's revised text.

The Ambassadors. 2nd ed. Edited by S. P. Rosenbaum. New York: W. W. Norton, 1994. A Norton Critical Edition.

The Ambassadors. Edited by Harry Levin. London: Penguin Books, 1986.

Other Works by Henry James

Literary Criticism: Essays on Literature, American Writers, English Writers. Edited by Leon Edel and Mark Wilson. New York: Library of America, 1984.

Literary Criticism: French Writers, Other European Writers, The Prefaces to the New York Edition. Edited by Leon Edel and Mark Wilson. New York: Library of America, 1984.

The Art of the Novel: Critical Prefaces by Henry James. Edited by Richard P. Blackmur. New York: Charles Scribner's Sons, 1934.

The Complete Notebooks of Henry James. Edited by Leon Edel and Lyall H. Powers. New York: Oxford University Press, 1987. Includes James's "Project of Novel" Scenario written for Harper's.

Selected Bibliography

The Letters of Henry James. Edited by Percy Lubbock. 2 volumes. New York: Charles Scribner's Sons, 1920.

Henry James Letters. Edited by Leon Edel. 4 volumes. Cambridge, Mass.: Harvard University Press, 1974–84.

The Correspondence of William James: William and Henry. Edited by Ignas K. Skrupskelis and Elizabeth M. Berkeley. Vols. 1–3. Charlottesville: University Press of Virginia, 1992–94.

Secondary Works

Books

Armstrong, Paul B. *The Phenomenology of Henry James.* Chapel Hill: University of North Carolina Press, 1983. Superb analysis of James and twentieth-century phenomenology.

Banta, Martha. *Henry James and the Occult.* Bloomington: Indiana University Press, 1972. Demonstrates James's imaginative use of the technical resources of the supernatural.

Barzun, Jacques. *A Stroll with William James.* New York: Harper & Row, 1983. Beautifully written meditation that includes commentary on Henry.

Beach, Joseph Warren. *The Method of Henry James.* New Haven, Conn.: Yale University Press, 1918. The pioneering analysis of James's technique.

Bellringer, Alan W. *The Ambassadors.* London: George Allen and Unwin, 1984. Balances information and criticism of the novel well.

Blackmur, R. P. *Studies in Henry James.* Edited by Veronica K. Makowsky. New York: New Directions, 1983. Collects all of Blackmur's important essays on James, including "The Loose and Baggy Monsters."

Bradbury, Nicola. *Henry James: The Later Novels.* Oxford: Clarendon Press, 1979. Best reader-response approach to the late novels.

Daugherty, Sarah B. *The Literary Criticism of Henry James.* Athens: Ohio University Press, 1981. Acute historical overview of the topic.

Dupee, F. W. *Henry James.* New York: William Sloan, 1951. A good short one-volume biography.

Edel, Leon. *The Life of Henry James.* 5 vols. Philadelphia: J. B. Lippincott, 1953–72. The definitive modern biography that is equally famous as a classic Freudian biography.

Fogel, Daniel M. *Henry James and the Structure of the Romantic Imagination.* Baton Rouge: Louisiana State University Press, 1981. Strong readings of the major-phase novels as embodying the Romantic structure of "spiral ascent."

Hocks, Richard A. *Henry James and Pragmatistic Thought: A Study in the Relationship between the Philosophy of William James and the Literary Art of Henry James.* Chapel Hill: University of North Carolina Press, 1974. Extensive analysis of parallelism in the brothers' intellectual relationship and of polarity in Henry.

Holly, Carol. *Intensely Family: The Inheritance of Family Shame and the Autobiographies of Henry James.* Madison: University of Wisconsin Press, 1995. Fine analysis of family psychodynamics embedded in James's autobiographies.

Horne, Philip. *Henry James and Revision.* Oxford: Clarendon Press, 1990. The most meticulous examination of James's revision process.

Johnson, Courtney Jr. *Henry James and the Evolution of Consciousness: A Study of "The Ambassadors."* East Lansing: Michigan State University Press, 1987. Claims that Strether achieves a state of enlightened "higher" consciousness of transcendence.

Kaplan, Fred. *Henry James: The Imagination of Genius.* New York: William Morrow and Co., 1992. Excellent recent biography that supplements Freudianism found in Edel.

Krook, Dorothea. *Henry James's "The Ambassadors": A Critical Study.* New York: AMS Press, Inc., 1996. A superb explanation of James's late style and a fine discussion of principal characters.

Lewis, R.W.B. *The Jameses: A Family Narrative.* New York: Farrar, Straus and Giroux, 1991. Extremely readable synthesis of work by other James family biographers.

Lubbock, Percy. *The Craft of Fiction.* New York: Charles Scribner's Sons, 1921. Early influential theory of fiction based on James's prefaces that uses *The Ambassadors* as a model.

Matthiessen, F.O. *The James Family, Including Selections from the Writings of Henry James, Senior, William, Henry, and Alice James.* New York: Alfred A. Knopf, 1947. Excellent collection of documentary materials with fine commentary.

McWhirter, David. *Desire and Love in Henry James.* Cambridge, England: Cambridge University Press, 1989. Thoughtful readings of the late novels: Strether exhibits desire but fails to achieve authentic love.

Nettles, Elsa. *James and Conrad.* Athens: University of Georgia Press, 1977. Contains a nice comparison of *The Ambassadors* with *Lord Jim.*

Perosa, Sergio. *Henry James and the Experimental Novel.* Charlottesville: University Press of Virginia, 1978. Traces James's experimentalism from the works of the middle period through the unfinished novels.

Rowe, John Carlos. *The Theoretical Dimension of Henry James.* Madison: University of Wisconsin Press, 1984. The magnum opus of James as a prism for contemporary theory.

Selected Bibliography

Tintner, Adeline R. *Henry James and the Lust of the Eyes*. Baton Rouge: Louisiana State University Press, 1993. Patented "iconographical" approach that includes *The Ambassadors* with Holbein and Titian.

Tuttleton, James W. *The Novel of Manners in America*. Chapel Hill: University of North Carolina Press, 1972. Strong study of the genre of *The Ambassadors*.

Walker, Pierre A. *Reading Henry James in French Cultural Contexts*. De Kalb: Northern Illinois University Press, 1995. Contains an excellent discussion of Strether vis-à-vis Balzac's *Louis Lambert*.

Wegelin, Christof. *The Image of Europe in Henry James*. Dallas: Southern Methodist University Press, 1958. Fine discussion of James's international juxtapositions throughout his fiction, including *The Ambassadors*.

Williams, Merle A. *Henry James and the Philosophical Novel*. Cambridge, England: Cambridge University Press, 1993. Rigorous analysis of later works from both deconstructive and phenomenological perspectives.

Yeazell, Ruth B. *Language and Knowledge in the Late Novels of Henry James*. Chicago: University of Chicago Press, 1976. Good on figurative language in the late novels.

Articles and Sections of Books

Abbot, Reginald. "The Incredible Floating Man: Henry James's Lambert Strether." *The Henry James Review* 11, 3 (Fall 1990): 176–88. Connects the novel's many floating and air images to fin de siècle art.

Armstrong, Paul B. "Reality and/or Interpretation in *The Ambassadors*." In *The Challenge of Bewilderment: Understanding and Representation in James, Conrad, and Ford*. Ithaca: Cornell University Press, 1987, 63–106. Brilliant hermeneutical and phenomenological reading of the novel.

Eliot, T.S. "A Prediction." In *Henry James: A Collection of Critical Essays*. Edited by Leon Edel. Englewood Cliffs, NJ: Prentice-Hall, 1963, 55–56. Compares James favorably with Dostoyevsky.

———. "Henry James: In Memory and The Hawthorne Aspect." In *The Shock of Recognition*. Edited by Edmund Wilson. New York: The Modern Library, 1943, 854–65. A reprinting of Eliot's seminal piece in the 1918 *Little Review*.

Greene, Graham. "The Private Universe." In *Henry James: A Collection of Critical Essays*. Edited by Leon Edel. Englewood Cliffs, NJ: Prentice-Hall, 1963, 111–22. Explores the roots of James's sense of evil.

Griffin, Susan M. "The Selfish Eye: Strether's Principles of Psychology." In *The Historical Eye: The Texture of the Visual in Late James*. Boston: Northeastern University Press, 1991, 33–56. Demonstrates that Strether's perception corresponds to William James's functionalist psychology.

Hocks, Richard A. "Quite the Best, 'All Round,' of All My Productions: The Multiple Versions of the Jamesian Germ for *The Ambassadors*." In *Biographies of Books: The Compositional Histories of Notable American Writings*. Edited by James Barbour and Tom Quirk. Columbia: University of Missouri Press, 1996, 110–30. Analyzes the permutations of the germ from James's notebooks through letters, the Scenario, the novel, and the preface to the New York Edition.

———. "The Several Canons of Henry James." *American Literary Realism* 27 (Spring 1991): 68–81. Situates the novel in the evolution of critical theory.

Hoople, Robin P. "Iconological Characterization in James's *The Ambassadors*." *American Literature* 60, 3 (1988): 416–32. Chad is the core "iconic" character that Strether ultimately sees aright.

Krook, Dorothea. "The Ambassadors: Two Types of Ambiguity." *Neophilologus* 74, 1 (1990): 148–55. Distinguishes between general obscurity and specific unresolved contradictions in the novel.

Matthiessen, F.O. "The Ambassadors." In *Henry James: The Major Phase*. New York: Oxford University Press, 1944, 18–41. Influential aesthetic criticism that revived interest in James's later work.

McGann, Jerome. "Revision, Rewriting, Rereading; or, 'An Error [Not] in *The Ambassadors*.' " *American Literature* 64 (March 1992): 95–110. Challenges with wit the conventional view that James reversed chapters 28 and 29 in the novel.

Posnock, Ross. "Going to Smash: Violence in *The Ambassadors*." In *The Trial of Curiosity*. New York: Oxford University Press, 1991, 221–49. Example of contemporary culture study. Strether and James anticipate the "politics of nonidentity."

Pound, Ezra. "Henry James." In *Instigations*. New York: Boni & Liveright, 1920, 106–67. Includes Pound's introduction to the Henry James issue of *Little Review* (August 1918).

Rivkin, Julie. "The Logic of Delegation in *The Ambassadors*." *PMLA* 101 (October 1986): 819–31. Sinuous discussion of the novel in terms of Derridian concept of "supplementarity."

Rowe, Joyce A. "Strether Unbound: The Selective Vision of Henry James's Ambassador." In *Equivocal Endings of Classic American Novels*. New York: Cambridge University Press, 1988, 75–99. A "darkish" reading of the ending: Strether's Emersonian moral idealism has been disillusioned.

Seidel, Michael. "The Lone Exile: James's *The Ambassadors* and *The American Scene*." In *Exile and the Narrative Imagination*. New Haven: Yale University Press, 1986, 131–63. Rich suggestive analysis relating James and Strether as exiles.

Steele, Meili. "Value and Subjectivity: The Dynamics of the Sentence in James's *The Ambassadors*." *Comparative Literature* 43, 2 (1991): 113–133. Semantic study with a good reading of the final scene between Strether and Maria Gostrey.

Tilford, J.E. Jr. "James the Old Intruder." *Modern Fiction Studies* 4 (Summer 1958): 157–64. One of the first to point out, pace Lubbock, that James is not entirely effaced in the novel.

Watt, Ian. "The First Paragraph of *The Ambassadors*: An Explication." *Essays in Criticism* 10 (July 1960): 250–74. Classic analysis of James's formal artistry.

Bibliographies and Scholarly Aids

Edel, Leon, and Dan H. Laurence. *A Bibliography of Henry James*. 3rd ed., rev. London: Rupert Hart-Davis, 1982. The definitive bibliography of primary works.

Fogel, Daniel M., ed. *A Companion to Henry James Studies*. Westport, Conn.: Greenwood Press, 1993. Authoritative essays by James scholars on each major aspect of his work.

Gale, Robert L. *A Henry James Encyclopedia*. New York: Greenwood Press, 1989. Thorough and comprehensive, with many excellent expanded entries.

McColgan, Kristian Pruitt. *Henry James, 1917–1959: A Reference Guide*. Boston: G. K. Hall, 1979.

Ricks, Beatrice. *Henry James: A Bibliography of Secondary Works*. Metuchen, N.J.: Scarecrow Press, 1975.

Scura, Dorothy M. *Henry James, 1960–1974: A Reference Guide*. Boston: G. K. Hall, 1979.

For studies of Henry James and of *The Ambassadors* published after 1974, see the Henry James chapter in the hardcover annual *American Literary Scholarship* (Durham: Duke University Press) and the annual volumes of the *MLA International Bibliography*.

Index

Index

Cervantes, Miguel de, *Don Quixote*, 51, 112

"central intelligence," 32, 33, 35, 36, 59, 64, 111

chiasmus, 130–32, 133

Cixous, Helene, 118

Colby, F. M., "In Darkest James," 139n. 1

Coleridge, Samuel Taylor, 102, 103, 104, 105, 109

comedy, 132; elements of, 110–17

Complete Notebooks of Henry James, The, 34–35, 50, 85, 99, 111, 122, 138n. 11, 146n. 1, 147n. 1, 149n. 1

Conrad, Joseph, 5, 6, 15, 47, 89; "An Appreciation," 6, 138n. 7, 139n. 1

consciousness, 4, 5, 11, 23, 24, 29–47, 49, 50, 58, 65, 67, 68, 73, 75, 85, 86, 101, 103, 106, 111, 113, 119, 133, 134, 144n. 19. *See also* stream-of-consciousness method

Cooper, F. T., "The Novelist's Omniscience and Some Recent Books," 139n. 1

Cooper, James Fenimore, 4

criticism. *See* literary criticism

Cross, Mary, 22; *Henry James: The Contingencies of Style*, 141n. 36

cultural criticism, 4, 5–6, 22–23, 71

Daisy Miller, 3, 9, 49, 52, 57, 112, 113, 119, 134

Daugherty, Sarah B., 20, 151; *The Literary Criticism of Henry James*, 140n. 23

deconstruction, 11–12, 104

"deputy," 32, 33, 35, 40, 59, 65, 123

Derrida, Jacques, 22, 23, 104, 118

Derridian supplementarity, 22

Descartes, René, 81

determinism, 10–11, 49, 85, 86, 107

Dewey, John, 81

Dickens, Charles, 4, 35

Dickinson, Emily, 88

Donadio, Stephen, 23; *Nietzche, Henry James, and the Artistic Will*, 142n. 39

Dostoyevsky, Fyodor, 7

Dreiser, Theodore, *Sister Carrie*, 51

dualism, 51, 71, 109

Dupee, F. W., 151

Eakin, Paul John, 23

Edel, Leon, 18, 20, 21, 146n. 23, 151, 155; *Henry James: The Untried Years, 1843–1870; The Conquest of London, 1870–1881; The Middle Years, 1882–1895; The Treacherous Years, 1895–1901; The Master, 1901–1916*, 139n. 14; *Library of Henry James, The*, 21, 141n. 32; *Life of Henry James, The*, 18

Eliot, George, 36

Eliot, T. S., 5, 7, 15, 19, 70, 74, 76, 132, 153; *Four Quartets*, 132; "Hawthorne Aspect, The," 139n. 3; "Henry James," 144n. 2; "In Memory," 139n. 3; "Prediction, A," 138n. 9

Elton, Oliver, "The Novels of Mr. Henry James," 139n. 1

Emerson, Ralph Waldo, 51, 54, 102

empiricism, 84

epic, 92. *See also* Homeric epic

episodic motif. *See* motif

epistemological bewilderment. *See* bewilderment

exile. *See* Homeric epic

existential morality, 67. *See also* morality

Index

Index

The Author

Richard A. Hocks is professor of English and Catherine Paine Middlebush Professor of Humanities at the University of Missouri, Columbia, where he teaches courses in American literature and in the two-year interdisciplinary humanities sequence. His books include *Henry James and Pragmatistic Thought* (nominated for the National Book Award in 1974) and *Henry James: A Study of the Short Fiction*. He also coedited, with J. Donald Crowley, the Norton Critical Edition of *The Wings of the Dove* by Henry James. Mr. Hocks is the author of scholarly articles on, among others, T. S. Eliot, Samuel Taylor Coleridge, Henry David Thoreau, Herman Melville, Henry James, Michael Polanyi, and Owen Barfield. A member of the editorial board of *The Henry James Review* and a past president of the Henry James Society, he writes or coordinates the Henry James chapter for *American Literary Scholarship, An Annual*.

The Editor

Robert Lecker is professor of English at McGill University in Montreal. He received his Ph.D. from York University. Professor Lecker is the author of numerous critical studies, including On the Line (1982), Robert Kroetch (1986), An Other I (1988), and Making It Real: The Canonization of English-Canadian Literature (1995). He is the editor of the critical journal Essays on Canadian Writing and of many collections of critical essays, most recent of which is Canadian Canons: Essays in Literary Value (1991). He is the founding and current general editor of Twayne's Masterwork Studies, and the editor of the Twayne World Authors Series on Canadian writers. He is also the general editor of G. K. Hall's Critical Essays on World Literature series.